An Investigation into Possible Applications of

FUZZY SET METHODS IN ACTUARIAL SCIENCE

KRZYSZTOF OSTASZEWSKI, A.S.A.

Society of Actuaries
475 North Martingale Road, Suite 800
Schaumburg, IL U.S.A. 60173-2226

HG 8781 .O84 1993
Ostaszewski, Krzysztof M., 1957–
An investigation into

NOTICE

Camera-ready copy prepared by the author using T_EX. The T_EX is a trademark of the American Mathematical Society.

Library of Congress Cataloging-in-Publication Data

    Ostaszewski, Krzysztof M., 1957–
        An investigation into possible applications of fuzzy sets methods
           in actuarial science / Krzysztof Ostaszewski.
        85 p. cm.
        Includes bibliographical references and index.
        ISBN 0–938959–27–1
        1. Insurance—Mathematics. 2. Fuzzy sets. I. Title.
    HG8781.O84 1993
    368′.01–dc20

                                  93–22360
                                    CIP

ISBN 0–938959–27–1

CONTENTS

PREFACE

This work was completed with support from a research grant awarded by the Society of Actuaries.

The author is most grateful for the reviews of this work provided by the Project Oversight Committee of the Society of Actuaries, by Professor Brian Schott, and by Edward A. Lew, the Chairman of the Research Management Committee. The author also wants to thank Professors Lotfi A. Zadeh and Ramohhan K. Ragade for discussing this work with him, and Mark G. Doherty, Director of Research of the Society of Actuaries, and Warren Luckner, Education Actuary of the Society, for the assistance and the patience offered to the author while this manuscript was being prepared.

Finally, I want to thank my wife, Patricia, for being patient, too.

ABOUT THE AUTHOR

Krzysztof M. Ostaszewski was born and grew up in the city of Lodz, Poland. At the University of Lodz, he received a master's degree in mathematics in 1980. After a year of graduate studies in mathematics and philosophy there, he started graduate work in mathematics at the University of Washington in Seattle. He received his Ph.D. in mathematics from the University of Washington in 1985.

Dr. Ostaszewski spent a year as a Visiting Assistant Professor at the University of California at Davis, and then in 1986 joined the faculty of the University of Louisville as an Assistant Professor. Since 1990, he has been coordinating the University of Louisville Actuarial Program, and in 1991, he became an Associate Professor of Mathematics.

Dr. Ostaszewski became a Chartered Financial Analyst in 1991 and an Associate of the Society of Actuaries in 1992. He has published extensively and in various areas. His credits include two research monographs in theoretical mathematics, which appeared as *Memoirs of the American Mathematical Society*, and papers in pure mathematics published in the *Proceedings of the American Mathematical Society, Springer Lecture Notes in Mathematics, Semigroup Forum*, and *Forum Mathematicum*. Dr. Ostaszewski's economic research has been published in *American Economic Review*. Other research works have appeared in *Springer Lecture Notes in Computer Science* and *Le Travail Humain*.

Dr. Ostaszewski also has written on the economic and political developments in Eastern Europe for *Reason and Liberty* and in an anthology on the subject. He has published five volumes of poetry, three of them in Polish and two in English.

INTRODUCTION

In actuarial work, Ruskin's statement: "The work of science is to substitute facts for appearances and demonstrations for impressions" is the guiding light for those in search of an accurate model of uncertain reality. The basic job of an actuary is to make conservative estimates of various risks in order to provide the public with a sound insurance system. What is proposed in this work is implementation of "non-precise", fuzzy reasoning methods in actuarial science. As strange as this idea may sound, fuzzy sets are not really as "fuzzy" and "imprecise" as they are sometimes presented to be. As stated in the *Principles of Actuarial Science* (Dicke *et al.*, 1991), adopted by the Society of Actuaries, "The stochastic aspect of a model may not be relevant to a given application; in such situations a deterministic model might be used." Fuzzy models may provide yet another alternative in creating mathematical models of phenomena which cannot be adequately described solely as stochastic.

What is the purpose of the now blossoming field of fuzzy set theory? It is designed to *model uncertainty*. As such, it should attract interest of actuaries. To arrive at precise statements, actuaries model various risk situations with the view of ascertaining their potential range of variability. The devotion to precision may cause suspicion towards the apparent vagueness of fuzzy sets. However, as Zimmerman (1991) points out "...there is nothing fuzzy about fuzzy set theory!". The mathematical methods of fuzzy sets are precise, and models used are based on the assumption that probability theory deals with only one of various types of uncertainty encountered by us. In as much as actuaries are in effect required to make long term projections into an increasingly fuzzy future, the concept of fuzzy sets may indeed be very helpful.

Smithson (1989) gives a unique review of the modern theories of uncertainty and ignorance. He writes " Not long ago, the dominant methods of coping with ignorance were to try eliminating it or absorbing it. The emerging frameworks now seem to have jettisoned the assumption that ignorance is ultimately reducible, and the new style is 'managerial' in the sense of attempting to understand, tolerate, or

1

even utilize certain types of ignorance." Fuzzy set theory is undoubtedly a part of those new emerging frameworks.

Black (1937) gave a classic account of the variety of uncertainties, by distinguishing among vagueness, nonspecificity, and ambiguity. The argument for inadequacy of probability theory in handling some types of uncertainty, especially the vagueness, is strengthened by the famous Ellsberg (1961) paradox: Imagine two urns, each containing 100 balls, of which the first one is known to contain 50 red balls and 50 black balls, without any further information about the contents of the other urn. If asked to bet on the color of a ball drawn from one of the urns, most people were found indifferent as to which color they would choose no matter whether the ball was drawn from the first or the second urn. On the other hand, Ellsberg found that if people were asked which urn they would prefer to use for betting on either color, they consistently favored the first urn (no matter what color they were asked to bet on). Smithson (1989) discusses the implications of this paradox for the classical axioms of probability, but for us it suffices to observe that it is the vagueness of the information given about the second urn that causes such unexpected reaction.

Klir and Folger (1988) further analyze the semantic context of the term *uncertain* and arrive at the conclusion that there are two main types of uncertainty, captured by the terms *vagueness* and *ambiguity* (Black's nonspecificity becomes a form of ambiguity in their classification). *Vagueness* is associated with the difficulty of making sharp or precise distinctions among the objects studied. *Ambiguity* is caused by situations where the choice between two or more alternatives is unspecified. Of course, one can easily imagine a combination of the above two factors. For example, when attempting to predict the future direction of interest rates, we are faced with the ambiguity of economic scenarios – we can have a recession accompanied by a drop in real rates, or accelerating inflation, or a combination of both. But even after the economic scenario is established, the exact rate of interest achieved by a given portfolio of investments is quite a vague concept, due to a combination of factors such as credit risk, default risk, timing of cash flows, and others.

2

While most actuaries rely on Kolmogorov's axiomatic approach to probability, and an increasing number are using a Bayesian approach, both of these models rest on the assumption that the outcome of a random event can be observed and identified with precision. All the physical sciences tend to reinforce that view. Any vagueness of observation is considered negligible, or not significant to the construction of the theoretical model. Dicke *et al.* (1991) state that "The uncertainty associated with a stochastic model has two distinct sources: the inherent variability of the phenomenon; and incomplete knowledge and/or inaccurate representation of the probabilities of alternative outcomes." Our work discusses inclusion of uncertainty due to vagueness in models applied by actuaries.

There may be several reasons for wanting to include models of a form of uncertainty other than randomness in actuarial science. One is that vagueness is unavoidable. Dicke *et al.* (1991) acknowledge that concept in their presentation of actuarial principles when they state "Most phenomena studied by actuaries are assumed to exhibit statistical regularity. In the real world, 'experiments' cannot be replicated precisely." If the degree of vagueness is so small that one can disregard it in the model, such ignorance of it is justifiable. We could make a case for that in the physical sciences. Paradoxically, however, the area of application of the physical sciences in engineering is the one where fuzzy set models are applied with greatest success. On the other hand, if the area studied is permanently "tainted" with imprecision of natural language, or human perception of the phenomena observed, vagueness becomes a major factor in any attempt to model or predict the course of events. Economics is an example of a science where the human perception of events is, in fact, a part of the events. The Consumer Confidence index is an attempt to measure a vague concept with precision. We believe it is only a matter of time before similar measurements utilizing fuzzy numbers are proposed. Utility theory also deals often with imprecision of human perception, and the actuarial principle of Diversity of Preferences (Dicke *et al.*, 1991) is an acknowledgement of that situation.

Thus vagueness and imprecision of human perception, and of the natural languages, is the first and foremost reason for applying fuzzy set theory in modeling uncertainty. But there is more. When the phenomena observed become so complex that exact measurement involving all features considered significant would take more than a lifetime, or longer than economically feasible for the study, mathematical precision is often abandoned in favor of more workable simple, but vague, "common sense" models. Thus, complexity of the problem may be another cause of vagueness. The choice of surplus for an insurance enterprise is an example of a problem of such a nature. One could choose its level in such a way as to estimate the probability of ruin to be less than, for example, 0.05, while maintaining competitive pricing. The 0.05 number is certain, but the probability it is being compared to is rather vague, due to the immense complexity of the problem. If the insurance firm were so certain of the value of its probability of ruin as not to consider it somewhat vague, why would anyone need experience adjustments?

Zadeh (1990) comments on vagueness resulting from complexity as follows: "When a point is reached where the cardinality of the class of subclasses exceeds the information handling capacity of the human brain, the boundaries of subclasses are forced to become imprecise and fuzziness becomes a manifestation of imprecision. (...) This is why (...) natural languages, which are much higher in level than programming languages, are fuzzy whereas programming languages are not."

Fuzzy set methods have their place not only in modeling vagueness, but also in dealing with ambiguity. It is clear that the concept of probability, by considering all possible outcomes of a random event, provides a mathematical base for dealing with ambiguity. But probability theory is not sufficiently general to handle all forms of ambiguity. In fact, Klir and Folger (1988) view probability as only a subset of the fuzzy measure theory, which they consider to be the general framework for dealing with ambiguity.

Three types of ambiguity are recognized by Klir and Folger (1988). The first one is the result of the size of the subsets that are designated by a fuzzy measure as prospective locations of the elements studied. The larger the subsets, the less specific the characterization. Klir and Folger (1988) call this *nonspecificity of evidence*.

4

The second type of ambiguity appears in the situation when disjoint subsets of a universe observed are designated as prospective locations of the object of concern. In this case, if the evidence focusing on one subset conflicts with evidence focusing on the other subsets, we speak of *dissonance in evidence*.

Finally, ambiguity may be associated with the number of subsets of the universe that are designated as possible locations of the object under consideration. Such a multitude of partially or totally conflicting evidence is refered to as *confusion in evidence*.

One may, therefore, conclude that probability theory models uncertainty only in the limited sense of its ambiguity meaning, and that fuzzy set methods developed naturally to fill the gap left by probability. Nevertheless, it should be acknowledged that some controversy concerning that conclusion remains. Kosko (1990) discusses it, and presents a strong defence for the feasibility of fuzzy models.

The history of fuzzy sets can be traced to works of philosophers interested in formal models of vagueness of natural languages. On June 5, 1920, at the 206th scientific meeting of the Polish Philosophical Society held in Lwów, Jan Łukasiewicz (also the creator of Polish notation, whose inverse version has been so successfully applied in computer science) delivered a talk on a three-valued logic. Łukasiewicz proposed a study of an alternative to the classical Aristotelian, or what is now called Boolean, logic, with only two truth-values, i.e., that of truth (associated with number 1), and falsehood (associated with number 0). Instead, Łukasiewicz considered multivalued logic, of which the simplest example would be that with three values: 0, representing a false statement, $\frac{1}{2}$, representing an uncertain statement, and 1, assigned to truth. One can, of course, envision another alternative – a logic in which a continuum of numbers in the interval $[0,1]$ represented possible truth-values of statements, from which the fuzzy set theory naturally develops.

Łukasiewicz (1920) published his work originally only in Polish (see also translation in McCall, 1967, pp. 15-18, also pp. 40-65), but then further developed his ideas in works written in German and English (Łukasiewicz, 1930, 1953, 1954). Łukasiewicz's theory was examined by philosophers in the context of *modal log-*

ic (Prior, 1953, also Von Wright, 1967, pp. 122-126). The relationship between Lukasiewicz's work and fuzzy sets is discussed by Giles (1976).

Post (1921), in the paper in which he introduced truth-tables for elementary logic, also suggested multivalued logic, apparently unaware of the Lukasiewicz's work.

Fuzzy set theory was created in the historic 1965 paper of Lotfi A. Zadeh. To present his basic idea, recall that a *characteristic function* of a subset E of a universe of discourse U is defined as

$$\chi_E(x) = \begin{cases} 1 & \text{if } x \in E \\ 0 & \text{if } x \in U \setminus E. \end{cases}$$

In other words, the characteristic function describes the membership of an element x in a set E. It equals one if x is a member of E, and 0 otherwise. There is nothing in between, as in Aristotelian logic there is nothing between truth and falsehood of the statement "x is an element of E".

Zadeh (1965) challenged the idea that membership in all sets considered behaves in the manner described above. One example would be the set of "tall people". We do consistently talk about the set of "tall people", yet understand that the concept used is not precise, and a person who is 5'11" is tall only to a certain degree, and yet such a person is not "not tall".

Zadeh (1965) writes "The notion of fuzzy set provides a convenient point of departure for the construction of a conceptual framework which parallels in many respects the framework used in the case of ordinary sets, but is more general than the latter and, potentially, may prove to have a much wider scope of applicability, particularly in the fields of pattern classification and information processing. Essentially, such a framework provides a natural way of dealing with problems in which the source of imprecision is the absence of sharply defined criteria of class membership rather than the presence of random variables."

Goguen (1967, 1969) gave an early generalization of Zadeh's ideas, while Zadeh (1969, 1973) and Bellman and Zadeh (1970) introduced their applications. Once introduced, fuzzy set theory quite rapidly found its way into direct applications in the engineering fields. The most spectacular ones came about as a result of utilizing fuzzy sets in decision theory, and in fuzzy industrial controllers. Bellman and Zadeh (1970) write: "(...) it is important to note that, in discourse between humans, fuzzy statements such as 'John is *several* inches taller tham Jim', 'x is *much* larger than y', 'Corporation X has a *bright* future', 'the stock market has suffered a *sharp* decline', convey information despite the imprecision of the meaning of the italicised words. In fact, it may be argued that the main distinction between human intelligence and machine intelligence lies in the ability of humans – an ability which present day computers do not possess – to manipulate fuzzy concepts and to respond to fuzzy instructions".

Mamdami (1974) provided a pioneering entry into the fuzzy controllers field. The first commercial product with a nature of a fuzzy control system shell was REVEAL (Jones, 1983, see also Graham, 1991), which grew out of earlier work by Jones in the area of financial modeling. The applications have, in fact, flourished. Schwartz (1990) gives an account of fascinating modern industrial applications of expert systems based on fuzzy sets. All of the expert systems use fuzzy approximate reasoning in a manner resembling human experts. Let us look at a couple of examples provided by Schwartz.

F.L. Smidth & Co. of Copenhagen, in conjunction with a research team from Queen Mary College in Denmark, designed in 1980 an expert system for controlling a kiln used in cement manufacturing. Rules used by the system to increase, decrease, or leave constant the rate of coal supplied to the kiln do not directly specify the amount of coal to be fed to the furnace, but rather use human-like instructions, such as *decrease coal feed*. The system is successfully applied at the Canada Cement Lafarge Plant in Ontario, Canada. For the discussion of the system, see Holmblad and Ostergaard (1983).

Mitsubishi Heavy Industries Inc. in cooperation with Togai InfraLogic Inc. of Irvine, California, have produced a fuzzy system for climate control, replacing traditional air-conditioning and heating control devices. The system is apparently quite succesful, as it improves temperature stability by a factor of two, while reducing energy consumption by more than 20%. Japanese companies are most actively pursuing applications of fuzzy expert systems. This includes the Sendai subway system, Panasonic's shower-head controller, or Yamaichi Securities use of fuzzy reasoning for stock market trading. Other successful applications of fuzzy expert systems are discussed by Graham (1991).

This book will present the basic concepts of the fuzzy set theory, including fuzzy sets, fuzzy measures, and approximate reasoning. In all cases, references for further studies, and for investigations of more advanced concepts, will be provided. Then, a review of fundamental concepts of actuarial science will be given from the perspective of possible applications of fuzzy set-theoretic methods. Although careful consideration has been given to all areas where uncertainty of a fuzzy nature arises, the summary may not be exhaustive. One can most certainly imagine this topic to be a subject of further numerous studies, both of theoretical and applied nature. In fact, one of the major functions of this work is to serve as an encouragement towards such work.

The mathematical concepts of the fuzzy set theory are presented in Chapter 1. The Introduction is meant to be less technical. Paradoxically, fuzzy set theory is not fuzzy, but mathematical and precise in nature, and sometimes may tend to appear technical in its details. We hope that the nontechnical parts of the book will serve as a motivation for reading of the more mathematical parts.

Chapter 1: BASIC MATHEMATICAL CONCEPTS

Let U stand for a universe of discourse; i.e., a certain set whose subsets are of interest to us. A *fuzzy subset* $\tilde{E}$ of U is defined by its *membership function* $\mu_E: U \to [0,1]$. For any $x \in U$, the value $\mu_E(x)$ specifies to what degree x belongs to the fuzzy set considered. We will write either (E, μ_E) for that fuzzy set or $\tilde{E}$, to distinguish from the notation E, generally denoting a standard set. The membership function is a generalization of a characteristic function of an ordinary set. Ordinary sets are called *crisp sets* in the fuzzy set theory, and considered a special case – a fuzzy set is crisp if, and only if, its membership function does not have fractional values.

Although a fuzzy set is introduced as an ordered pair consisting of a set and the membership function, we can see easily that, once the universe of discourse is fixed, it is the membership function which defines the set completely. Kosko (1990) stresses that fuzzy sets are in fact points in the cube $[0,1]^U$; i.e., instead of the traditional power-set (the set of all subsets) identificiation with $\{0,1\}^U$, we get the identification of the set of all fuzzy subsets of U with the set $[0,1]^U$, the "filled out" version of $\{0,1\}^U$. This allows Kosko to visualize fuzzy sets as points in a cube, generally infinite-dimensional (although applications of fuzzy sets theory usually bring us to study of finite fuzzy sets, so the corresponding cube is finite-dimensional).

In view of the above definition, we can see that every element of the universe U comes equipped with its degree of membership in a fuzzy set $\tilde{E}$, that degree of membership being represented by the value of its membership function. One can say that if, for example, $\mu_E(x) = 0.6$, then we are 60% certain that the element x belongs to the fuzzy set $\tilde{E}$. This is not meant to represent *a priori* uncertainty which can be removed by an experiment (such is the nature of randomness), but rather vagueness, or at least ambiguity which cannot be represented by a probabilistic model.

9

We define the α-*cut* of a fuzzy set $\tilde{E}$ as

$$E_\alpha = \{x \in U : \mu_E(x) \geq \alpha\}.$$

It is very important to observe that an α-cut of a fuzzy set is a crisp (i.e., ordinary) set. Therefore, α-cuts provide a natural way of transforming a fuzzy set (e.g., an outcome of an approximate reasoning procedure, or another application of fuzzy methodology) into a crisp set, which can then be used directly in the same way as an ordinary set. For example, if one wants to determine the set of high risks among the proposed insureds, and a fuzzy procedure gives that set as fuzzy $\tilde{E}$, a 0.8-cut, or a 0.9-cut would serve very well as the final outcome of the procedure.

An α-cut can be viewed as an aggregation of level sets. An α-level in a fuzzy set $\tilde{E}$ is

$$\Lambda_\alpha = \{x \in U : \mu_E(x) = \alpha\}.$$

One can easily see that

$$E_\alpha = \bigcup_{\beta \geq \alpha} \Lambda_\beta.$$

The set difference $E_\alpha \setminus \Lambda_\alpha$ is called *strong α-cut*. The strong 0-cut of a fuzzy set is called the *support* of $\tilde{E}$.

As a simple example of applicability of the above concepts, let us consider the set $\tilde{A}$ defined by Zimmerman (1991), p. 12, "comfortable type of a house for a four-person family", where the universe of discourse $X = \{1, 2, 3, 4, 5, 6, 7, 8, 9, 10\}$ is the set of available types of houses described by the number of bedrooms in a house. Zimmerman defines

$$\tilde{A} = \{(1, 0.2), (2, 0.5), (3, 0.8), (4, 1.0), (5, 0.7), (6, 0.3), (7, 0), (8, 0), (9, 0), (10, 0)\},$$

where the pairs are elements of X with their membership degrees in $\tilde{A}$ assigned to them. In this case,

$$A_{0.8} = \{3, 4\},$$

while

$$\Lambda_{0.8} = \{3\}.$$

A fuzzy set $\tilde{E}$ is called *normal* if there exists an $x \in U$ such that $\mu_E(x) = 1$, otherwise $\tilde{E}$ is called subnormal. This, of course, is equivalent to saying that a normal fuzzy set is a set whose 1-cut is nonempty.

Most fuzzy sets studied in this work will be numerical; i.e., their elements will be either real or natural numbers, or vectors whose coordinates are such numbers. We will denote the set of real numbers by $\mathbf{R}$ and the set of natural numbers by $\mathbf{N}$ (i.e., $\mathbf{N} = \{1, 2, 3, \ldots\}$). A fuzzy subset $\tilde{E}$ of $\mathbf{R}$ is *convex* if for each $\theta \in (0, 1)$ and $x, y \in \mathbf{R}$

$$\mu_E\left(\theta x + (1 - \theta)y\right) \geq \min\left(\mu_E(x), \mu_E(y)\right).$$

A fuzzy subset $\tilde{E}$ of $\mathbf{R}$ which is normal, convex, and such that μ_E is continuous and vanishes outside some interval $[a, b] \subset \mathbf{R}$ is called a *fuzzy number*. Any standard real number (i.e., an element of $\mathbf{R}$) can be viewed as a subset of $\mathbf{R}$ whose characteristic function is a limit of a sequence of membership functions of fuzzy numbers, with each of the elements of the sequence attaining its maximum at the standard real number considered. Because of that, standard real numbers are considered a special case of fuzzy numbers, and referred to as a *crisp numbers*.

The fundamental tool of the study of fuzzy sets is the following theorem due to Zadeh (1965). It provides a method of extending functions defined on crisp sets to fuzzy sets. We state it in the generalized form given by Zadeh (1975) (see also Dubois and Prade, 1980).

Theorem. (The Extension Principle) *If f is a mapping from a universe U which is a Cartesian product of universes U_1, U_2, ..., U_n, to a universe V, and $\tilde{A}_1$, $\tilde{A}_2$, ..., $\tilde{A}_n$ are fuzzy subsets of U_1, U_2, ..., U_n, respectively, then f maps the n-tuple $(\tilde{A}_1, \tilde{A}_2, ..., \tilde{A}_n)$, into a fuzzy subset $\tilde{B}$ of V in the following manner: if $f^{-1}(\{y\}) \neq \emptyset$ then*

$$\mu_B(y) = \sup\{\min\left(\mu_{A_1}(x_1), \ldots, \mu_{A_n}(x_n)\right) : (x_1, \ldots, x_n) \in f^{-1}(\{y\})\}$$

and $\mu_B(y) = 0$ otherwise.

11

We will give a simple application of the Extension Principle to illustrate it:

Let X and Y be two distinct and disjoint universes, both subsets of $\mathbf{R}$, where

$$X = \{x_1, x_2, x_3\}$$

and

$$Y = \{y_1, y_2, y_3\}.$$

Let $\tilde{A}$ be a fuzzy subset of X with $\mu_A(x_i) = \frac{i}{3}$, and $\tilde{B}$ be a fuzzy subset of Y with $\mu_B(y_i) = \frac{i+1}{4}$. Consider a function $f: X \times Y \to \mathbf{R}$ defined as

$$f(x_i, y_j) = a_{ij},$$

where $[a_{ij}]$ is a 3×3 real-valued matrix with $a_{ij} = a_{ji} = |i - j|$. In other words, we have

$$\mu_A(x_1) = \frac{1}{3}, \quad \mu_B(y_1) = \frac{1}{2},$$
$$\mu_A(x_2) = \frac{2}{3}, \quad \mu_B(y_2) = \frac{3}{4},$$
$$\mu_A(x_3) = 1, \quad \mu_B(y_3) = 1,$$

and the values assigned to pairs (x_i, y_j), $i = 1, 2, 3$, $j = 1, 2, 3$, are given by the table

	y_1	y_2	y_3
x_1	0	1	2
x_2	1	0	1
x_3	2	1	0

Then the fuzzy image set $f\left(\tilde{A}, \tilde{B}\right) = \tilde{C}$ has

$$\mu_C(0) = \max\left(\min\left(\frac{1}{3}, \frac{1}{2}\right), \min\left(\frac{2}{3}, \frac{3}{4}\right), \min(1, 1)\right) = 1,$$

$$\mu_C(1) = \max\left(\min\left(\frac{2}{3}, \frac{1}{2}\right), \min\left(\frac{1}{3}, \frac{3}{4}\right), \min\left(1, \frac{3}{4}\right), \min\left(\frac{2}{3}, 1\right)\right) = \frac{3}{4},$$

$$\mu_C(2) = \max\left(\min\left(1, \frac{1}{2}\right), \min\left(\frac{1}{3}, 1\right)\right) = \frac{1}{2}.$$

The Extension Principle can be used to generalize any crisp concept to fuzzy sets. It should be admitted that an unfortunate side-effect of it is the existence of publications based on the principle of "fuzzification" of known results of standard mathematics, without genuine need for fuzzy analogues. We will make a sincere effort in this work to avoid such phenomena.

We will now proceed to define basic operations on fuzzy sets.

Complement: If $\tilde{A} = (A, \mu_A)$ is a fuzzy subset of U, then its complement $\tilde{A}^c$ is a fuzzy subset of U with the membership function

$$\mu_{A^c}(x) = 1 - \mu_A(x), \ x \in U.$$

The above is not the only acceptable definition of the complement, although it is the most natural one. Klir and Folger (1988) specify two axiomatic requirements for a fuzzy complement operation. A complement of a fuzzy set $\tilde{E}$ is specified by a function $c: [0, 1] \rightarrow [0, 1]$ such that $c(0) = 1$, $c(1) = 0$ (this makes the function c a generalization of the complement of crisp sets), and c is monotonic nonincreasing. In most applications two more requirements are added: that c is a continuous function, and that c is involutive (it is its own inverse), i.e., $c(c(x)) = x$ for all $x \in [0, 1]$. Once a function c is specified, the complement of a fuzzy set $\tilde{E}$ with a membership function μ_E is defined to have the membership function $\mu_{E^c}(x) = c(\mu_E(x))$. Klir and Folger (1988) discuss two classes of complement operators which have been successfully implemented: the *Sugeno class* is defined as

$$c_\lambda(x) = \frac{1 - x}{1 + \lambda x},$$

where $\lambda \in (-1, +\infty)$ is a parameter, and the *Yager class*

$$c_\omega(x) = (1 - x^\omega)^{\frac{1}{\omega}},$$

where $\omega \in (0, +\infty)$ is a parameter.

Union: The union of (A, μ_A) and (B, μ_B) is the fuzzy set (C, μ_c) such that

$$\mu_C(x) = \max(\mu_A(x), \mu_B(x)).$$

In general, the union is specified by a function

$$u: [0, 1] \times [0, 1] \rightarrow [0, 1]$$

13

which produces the values of the membership function of $\tilde{A} \cup \tilde{B}$ via

$$\mu_{A \cup B}(x) = u\left(\mu_A(x), \mu_B(x)\right).$$

The following axioms are required of the function u (Klir and Folger, 1988):

Axiom u1: $u(0,0) = 0$, $u(0,1) = u(1,0) = u(1,1) = 1$; that is, u behaves as the classical union with crisp sets (*boundary conditions*).

Axiom u2: $u(x,y) = u(y,x)$; that is, u is *commutative*.

Axiom u3: If $x \leq x'$ and $y \leq y'$, then $u(x,y) \leq u(x',y')$; that is, u is *monotonic*.

Axiom u4: $u\left(u(x,y),z\right) = u\left(x,u(y,z)\right)$; that is, u is *associative*.

Axiom u5: u is a continuous function.

Axiom u6: $u(x,x) = x$; that is, u is *idempotent*.

The first four axioms are called the *axiomatic skeleton for fuzzy set unions*. It should be noted, however, that the last two axioms assure us of preservation of very natural properties of unions – Axiom u5 says that a small change in membership in one of the sets gives a relatively small change in the membership in the union, while Axiom u6 says that a union of a set with itself yields precisely the same set.

It is clear that the standard definition of a union given above satisfies the Axioms u1–u6. A more general class of operators u for which the Axioms also hold is the *Yager class*:

$$u_\omega(x,y) = \min\left(1, \left(a^\omega + b^\omega\right)^{\frac{1}{\omega}}\right),$$

where $\omega \in (0, +\infty)$ is a parameter.

Intersection: The intersection of (A, μ_A) and (B, μ_B) is defined as the fuzzy set (C, μ_c) such that

$$\mu_C = \min\left(\mu_A(x), \mu_B(x)\right).$$

Again, this classical definition can be extended by specifying the fuzzy intersection axioms. The *general fuzzy intersection* of two fuzzy sets A and B is specified by a function (Klir and Folger, 1988)

$$i \colon [0,1] \times [0,1] \to [0,1]$$

14

in such a way that

$$\mu_{A \cap B}(x) = i(\mu_A(x), \mu_B(x))$$

and i satisfies the following axioms:

Axiom i1: $i(1,1) = 1$, $i(0,1) = i(1,0) = i(0,0) = 0$; that is, i behaves as the classical intersection with crisp sets (*boundary conditions*).

Axiom i2: $i(x,y) = i(y,x)$; that is, i is *commutative*.

Axiom i3: If $x \leq x'$ and $y \leq y'$, then $i(x,y) \leq i(x',y')$; that is, i is *monotonic*.

Axiom i4: $i(i(x,y),z) = i(x,i(y,z))$; that is, i is *associative*.

Axiom i5: i is a continuous function.

Axiom i6: $i(x,x) = x$; that is, i is *idempotent*.

Again, the Axioms i1–i4 are refered to as the *axiomatic skeleton for fuzzy set intersections*, but Axioms i5 and i6 are of significance for reasons analogous to those stated above for Axioms u5 and u6. The classical intersection satisfies all of the axioms, and so does the general *Yager class* of intersection operators:

$$i_\omega(x,y) = 1 - \min\left(1, ((1-x)^\omega + (1-y)^\omega)^{\frac{1}{\omega}}\right),$$

where $\omega \in (0, +\infty)$ is a parameter.

The axioms for generalized fuzzy union and fuzzy intersection presented above fall within the framework of the study of the so called *T-norms* and *T-conorms*. The triangular norm (*T*-norm) and the triangular conorm (*T*-conorm) originated in the work of Menger (1942) concerning certain aspects of probabilistic metric spaces (see also Schweizer and Sklar, 1982). Höhle (1978), Alsina, Trillas and Valverde (1983) showed that *T*-norms and *T*-conorms can be used to generalize the definition of fuzzy union and fuzzy intersection, and consequently to define alternative rules of fuzzy inference.

A *T-norm* (Gupta and Qi, 1991) is a function $T : [0,1] \times [0,1] \to [0,1]$ such that

T1. $T(x,y) = T(y,x)$; i.e., T is *commutative*.

T2. $T(x,y) \leq T(x,z)$ if $y \leq z$; i.e., T is *monotonic*.

T3. $T(x,T(y,z)) = T(T(x,y),z)$; i.e., T is *associative*.

$T4.$ $T(x, 1) = x.$

A T-norm is *Archimedean* if it is a continuous function and $T(x, x) < x$ for all $x \in [0, 1]$.

A dual concept is that of a T-conorm (Gupta and Qi, 1991) which is defined as a function $T^*: [0, 1] \times [0, 1] \to [0, 1]$ such that

$T^*1.$ $T^*(x, y) = T^*(y, x)$; i.e., T^* is *commutative*.

$T^*2.$ $T^*(x, y) \leq T^*(x, z)$ if $y \leq z$; i.e., T^* is *monotonic*.

$T^*3.$ $T^*(x, T^*(y, z)) = T^*(T^*(x, y), z)$; i.e., T^* is *associative*.

$T^*4.$ $T(x, 0) = x.$

A T-conorm is *Archimedean* if it is continuous and $T^*(x, x) > x$ for $x \in [0, 1]$.

Both T-norms and T-conorms are included in the class of general T-*operators* which also contain the *negation functions* defined as functions $N: [0, 1] \to [0, 1]$ such that $N(0) = 1$, $N(1) = 0$, and N is nonincreasing. A negation function is *strict* if it is continuous and strictly decreasing. A strict negation function is involutive if it equals its own inverse function.

Gupta and Qi (1991, Sections 3 and 4) give a list of T-operators which have been studied in the theory of fuzzy sets and utilized in applications, and discuss their properties. The T-operators are used in generating fuzzy set operations which are of importance in applications involving inferences concerning several fuzzy sets. The most important applications involve the expert systems using fuzzy inference rules. Before we proceed to explain the fundamental concepts of fuzzy inreference, we need to define fuzzy relations.

If U and V are two universes, a fuzzy subset $\tilde{R}$ of the Cartesian product $U \times V$ is called a *fuzzy relation* on $U \times V$. Zimmerman (1991) gives an example of a fuzzy relation $\tilde{R}$ = "considerably larger than" on $\mathbf{R} \times \mathbf{R}$ with the membership function

$$\mu_R(x, y) = \begin{cases} 0 & \text{for } x \leq y, \\ \frac{(x-y)}{10y} & \text{for } y < x \leq 11y, \\ 1 & \text{for } x > 11y. \end{cases}$$

This definition of "considerably larger than" says that if $x > 11y$ then x is definitely considerably larger than y, otherwise the statement is true only to a certain degree, except when $x \leq y$ – in that situation the statement is definitely false.

Fuzzy inference is defined as deduction of new conclusions from the given information in the form of 'IF-THEN' rules in which both antecedents and consequents are given by fuzzy sets. Fuzzy inference is the basis for the theory of *approximate reasoning* as developed by Zadeh (1973). In much of human reasoning, the form of it is approximate rather than exact, in the sense that the logic used only resembles that of firm Aristotelian standards. Consider a shopper looking at tomatoes in a grocery store, thinking: "A red tomato is ripe. This one is more red than the other ones. Therefore it is more ripe than the other ones". That style of thinking is not limited to shoppers, of course. Countless industrial processes, or management decisions are handled in a similar manner, with experience of the decision maker being the creator of the approximate rule of reasoning followed. This is not necessarily a negative. It may be completely fruitless to try to analyze all details of a problem when an approximate solution, or a simple rule of thumb, are acceptable. Fuzzy sets are applicable in such situations.

The fundamental concept of fuzzy models of approximate reasoning is that of a *linguistic variable*, defined by Zadeh (1975). Simply stated, a linguistic variable is a variable taking on values being words (or sentences) of a natural (or artificial) language.

A typical form of fuzzy inference is as follows:

Implication: if x is A, then y is B

Premise: x is A'

———————————————————

Conclusion: y is B'

where x and y are linguistic variables, and A, A', B, and B' are fuzzy sets representing linguistic labels (values of linguistic variables) over the corresponding universes of discourse.

In the implementation of fuzzy control methods, the first step is to collect information from an experienced human operator who provides a verbal description of the expert knowledge about the process in the form of numerous 'IF-THEN' rules, say

$$\text{If } x \text{ is } A_1, \text{ then } y \text{ is } B_1$$

$$\text{If } x \text{ is } A_2, \text{ then } y \text{ is } B_2$$

$$\ldots$$

$$\text{If } x \text{ is } A_N, \text{ then } y \text{ is } B_N.$$

It is understood that values of the linguistic variables x and y can be represented here by fuzzy subsets of the universes considered, with U being the universe for values of x and V being the universe for the values of y. The implication relation between each A_i and the corresponding B_i is then represented by a fuzzy relation $R_{A_i \to B_i}$ on the universe $U \times V$ whose membership function is determined by an appropriate T-norm via

$$\mu_{R_{A_i \to B_i}}(x,y) = T\left(\mu_{A_i}(x), \mu_{B_i}(y)\right), \ x \in U, y \in V.$$

The above is refered to as the Mamdami implication function. Gupta and Qi (1991) identify also two other implication functions defined by Zadeh, given by

$$\mu_{R_{A_i \to B_i}}(x,y) = T^*\left(T\left(\mu_{A_i}(x), \mu_{B_i}(y)\right), N\left(\mu_{A_i}(x)\right)\right),$$

and

$$\mu_{R_{A_i \to B_i}}(x,y) = T^*\left(\mu_{B_i}(y), N\left(\mu_{A_i}(x)\right)\right),$$

where T is an appropriate T-norm, T^* is an appropriate T-conorm, and N is an appropriate negation function.

Recall that a T-conorm is associative and commutative, and as a result of that we can introduce the notation

$$T^{*N}_{i=1}(a_i) = T^*\left(T^*\left(\ldots T^*\left(T^*\left(a_1, a_2\right), a_3\right), \ldots\right), a_N\right).$$

The overall fuzzy relation R describing the expert knowledge is then defined via

$$\mu_R(x,y) = T^{*N}_{i=1}\left(\mu_{R_{A_i \to B_i}}(x,y)\right).$$

Given an antecedent A', i.e., a control condition, and the above fuzzy relation, the membership function of a consequent B' is determined by the *compositional rule of inference* $B' = A' \circ R$, defined by

$$\mu_{B'}(y) = \sup_x \; T\left(\mu_{A'}(x), \mu_R(x,y)\right).$$

The above construction is the most general description of compositional fuzzy inference. Simpler methods do exist – one can, for example, abandon the reference to general T-norms and T-conorms, and use the classical definitions of union and intersection to generate fuzzy rules of inference. We will illustrate that classical approach in Chapter 6, as applied to risk classification.

The basis of the probability theory traditionally used by actuaries is the measure theory as formulated originally in the doctoral dissertation of Henri Lebesgue (1902). Although this is a powerful tool in dealing with uncertainty of the ambiguity type, the fuzzy set theory proposes a generalization of it, to describe ambiguity when combined with vagueness, or ambiguity combined with excessive complexity. A *fuzzy measure* on a universe U is defined by a function

$$g : \mathcal{P}(U) \to [0,1],$$

where $\mathcal{P}(U)$ is the set of all subsets of U (the powerset of U) such that $g(\emptyset) = 0$, $g(U) = 1$, and g satisfies the following two conditions:

(i) (*Monotonicity*) If $A, B \in \mathcal{P}(U)$ and $A \subset B$, then $g(A) \leq g(B)$.

(ii) (*Continuity*) If $\{A_n\}_{n \in \mathbf{N}}$ is a sequence of subsets of U such that either $A_1 \subset A_2 \subset \ldots$ or $A_1 \supset A_2 \supset \ldots$ (i.e., the sequence is monotonic) then

$$\lim_{n \to \infty} g\left(A_n\right) = g\left(\lim_{n \to \infty} A_n\right).$$

One may also define a fuzzy measure on a field of subsets of U, or a σ-field (as in the case of classical probability measures), but the above is the most commonly used definition (see also Klir and Folger, 1988, or Zimmerman, 1991).

A *belief measure* is a function $Bel: \mathcal{P}(U) \to [0,1]$ which is a fuzzy measure such that for any $n \in \mathbf{N}$, and any n-element collection A_1, A_2, ..., A_n of crisp subsets of U we have

$$Bel\left(A_1 \cup A_2 \cup \ldots \cup A_n\right) \geq$$
$$\sum_{i=1}^{n} Bel(A_i) - \sum_{i<j} Bel\left(A_i \cap A_j\right) + \ldots + (-1)^{n+1} Bel\left(A_1 \cap A_2 \cap \ldots A_n\right).$$

A fuzzy measure $Pl: \mathcal{P}(U) \to [0,1]$ for which the above holds with the inequeality reversed; i.e.,

$$Pl\left(A_1 \cup A_2 \cup \ldots \cup A_n\right) \leq$$
$$\sum_{i=1}^{n} Pl(A_i) - \sum_{i<j} Pl\left(A_i \cap A_j\right) + \ldots + (-1)^{n+1} Pl\left(A_1 \cap A_2 \cap \ldots A_n\right)$$

is called a *plausibility measure*.

Belief and plausibility measures, and other generalized fuzzy measures are used to describe the degree of evidence supporting the claim that a specific element of U belongs to the set A, but not to any special subset of A, or the degree to which we believe that such a claim is warranted.

Zadeh (1978) introduced the concept of a *possibility measure*. It is defined as a function $\Pi: \mathcal{P} \to [0,1]$ such that $\Pi(\emptyset) = 0$, $\Pi(U) = 1$, $\Pi(A) \leq \Pi(B)$ whenever $A \subset B$, and if $\{A_t\}_{t \in \mathcal{T}}$ is an arbitrary indexed family of subsets of U then

$$\Pi\left(\bigcup_{t \in \mathcal{T}} A_t\right) = \sup_{t \in \mathcal{T}} \Pi\left(A_t\right).$$

Puri and Ralescu (1982) show that a possibility measure may not be a fuzzy measure, but if the universe considered is finite and Π is surjective (an "onto" mapping), then every possibility measure is a fuzzy measure.

Every possibility measure is uniquely determined by its *possibility distribution function* $f: U \to [0,1]$, and we have

$$\Pi(A) = \sup_{x \in A} f(x) \text{ for } A \subset U, \text{ and}$$
$$f(x) = \Pi\left(\{x\}\right) \text{ for } x \in U.$$

We have used above the standard notation $\mathcal{P}(U)$ to represent the class of all crisp subsets of the universe U. As the natural generalization, let $\tilde{\mathcal{P}}(U)$ be the class of all fuzzy subsets of the universe U. Another interesting concept is that of a *measure of fuzziness* (obviously not to be confused with a fuzzy measure defined above). A measure of fuzziness is defined as a function $f: \tilde{\mathcal{P}}(U) \to \mathbf{R}$ which satisfies the following axioms:

Axiom f1. $f\left(\tilde{A}\right) = 0$ if, and only if, $\tilde{A}$ is a crisp set.

Axiom f2. If $\mu_A(x) \le \mu_B(x)$ for every $x \in U$ then $f\left(\tilde{A}\right) \le f\left(\tilde{B}\right)$.

Axiom f3. $f\left(\tilde{A}\right)$ is maximum if, and only if, $\mu_A(x) = \frac{1}{2}$ for all $x \in U$.

Axiom f4. $f\left(\tilde{A}\right) = f\left(\tilde{A}^c\right)$ where $\tilde{A}^c$ is the fuzzy complement of $\tilde{A}$.

De Luca and Termini (1972) use the above approach for finite fuzzy sets and define the *entropy as a measure of fuzziness* via:

$$f\left(\tilde{A}\right) = H\left(\tilde{A}\right) + H\left(\tilde{A}^c\right),$$

with

$$H\left(\tilde{A}\right) = -K \sum_{i=1}^{n} \mu_A(x_i) \ln\left(\mu_A(x_i)\right)$$

where $x_1, x_2, \ldots, x_n$ are the elements where μ_A assumes positive values, and K is a positive constant.

If *Shannon's function* $S(x) = -x \ln x - (1-x)\ln(1-x)$ is used, the above simplifies to

$$f\left(\tilde{A}\right) = K \sum_{i=1}^{n} S\left(\mu_A(x_i)\right).$$

The above approach is not a universally accepted one. The obvious purpose of introducing a concept of measure of fuzziness is to indicate the degree of fuzziness of a fuzzy set. Yager (1979) proposes an alternative measure of fuzziness defined in such a way as to measure the lack of distinction between a fuzzy set $\tilde{A}$ and its fuzzy complement. For a fuzzy set $\tilde{A}$ such that μ_A is positive only on a finite set $Z = \{x_1, x_2, \ldots, x_n\}$, and a parameter $p \in \mathbf{N}$, we define the distance between $\tilde{A}$ and its fuzzy complement as

$$D_p\left(\tilde{A}, \tilde{A}^c\right) = \left(\sum_{i=1} |\mu_A(x_i) - \mu_{A^c}(x_i)|^p\right)^{\frac{1}{p}}.$$

The measure of fuzziness is then defined as

$$f_p\left(\tilde{A}\right) = 1 - \frac{D_p\left(\tilde{A}, \tilde{A}^c\right)}{D_p\left(Z, Z^c\right)}.$$

This measure, although based on a different approach, does satisfy the Axioms f1–f4 above.

Measures of fuzziness are an alternative to two classical measures of uncertainty – the *Hartley information*, and the *Shannon entropy*. Klir and Folger (1988) discuss the relationship of various measures of uncertainty in Chapter 5 of their book.

With the hope that the reader has gained some familiarity with the basic concepts of fuzzy sets theory we will now proceed to review possible applicability of that theory in certain fundamental concepts of actuarial science, following the classification of those concepts in the work of Trowbridge (1989).

Chapter 2: ECONOMICS OF RISK

The basic economic principle which is the foundation of insurance is utility. Insurance exists because of the risk aversion of the decision makers, and the concavity of the utility function of a typical decision maker. It could be argued that due to constantly changing perception of the world, a decision maker does not, in fact, have an unchanging and certain utility function, but an uncertain, varying one, with uncertainty of utility assigned to an outcome possibly modeled by fuzzy sets.

Ponsard (1979, 1985, see also 1981, 1982) gave the pioneer study of fuzziness of consumer's preferences. The axiomatic structure of fuzzy utility is studied by Mathieu-Nicot (1986). We will present the basic concepts of Mathieu-Nicot's work here, with some discussion.

Denote by $\mathcal{S}$ the class of the states of nature. We assume that there is a probability measure P defined for each state of nature. Let $\mathcal{X}$ be the set of results. Recall that the set of *actions* (or *decisions*) $\mathcal{D}$ is, in general, defined as a subset of $\mathcal{X}^{\mathcal{S}}$.

A *weak σ-field* $\mathcal{A}$ is defined as a class of fuzzy subsets of a universe U such that

(i) $\emptyset, U \in \mathcal{A}$;

(ii) If $\tilde{A} \in \mathcal{A}$ and $\tilde{B} \in \mathcal{A}$ then $\tilde{A} \cap \tilde{B} \in \mathcal{A}$;

(iii) If $\{\tilde{A}_n\}_{n \in \mathbb{N}}$ is a sequence of elements of $\mathcal{S}$ then $\bigcup_{n \in \mathbb{N}} \tilde{A}_n \in \mathcal{A}$.

To characterize the decision of the decision maker in fuzzy terms, we assume that a weak σ-field $\mathcal{H}$ of fuzzy subsets of $\mathcal{D}$ is given, with each element $\tilde{H}$ of $\mathcal{H}$ considered to be a fuzzy set.

Fuzzy, or crisp, utility value $U(\tilde{H}, S)$ is assigned to each pair $\tilde{H} \in \mathcal{H}$, $S \in \mathcal{S}$, with fuzzy expected utility of a decision $\tilde{H}$ defined as

$$W(H) = \sum_{S \in \mathcal{S}} U(\tilde{H}, S) P(S).$$

Mathieu-Nicot (1986) gives four axioms of fuzzy utility, concerning the existence of preference order, fuzzy mixture operation properties, independence of the order structure, and "existence of lottery tickets". An interested reader is refered to that paper for the more technical discussion.

Consider now the simplest form of the fuzzy utility question. Let

$$S = \{s_1, s_2, \ldots, s_q\}$$

be the set of states of nature, and $\mathcal{H} = \{h_1, h_2, \ldots, h_n\}$ be the set of actions that can be performed. If we denote the utility of the outcome of the combination of the state of nature s_i and the decision h_j by $u_{i,j}$, then given the state of nature s_{i_0}, the best action is h_{j_0} such that

$$u_{i_0, j_0} = \max_{1 \leq j \leq n} u_{i,j}.$$

If the states of nature become fuzzy, each utility will necessarily become fuzzy. The idea is as follows: the set S remains the universe of discourse for the states of nature, but its *fuzzy subsets* are now possible states of nature, each state $\tilde{S}$ being defined by a function $\mu_S : S \to [0,1]$. Then the utility of an action h_j in the state $\tilde{S}$ is $\tilde{U}(\tilde{S}, h_j)$ assigning to each $u_{i,j}$ membership value $\mu_S(s_i)$. It is also possible to consider fuzzy states of nature and fuzzy actions, with an additional principle (e.g., the maximin principle of Zadeh, 1965) determining the membership function values.

Under such construction the question of ranking of fuzzy utilities naturally arises. The most standard approach comes from comparison of fuzzy numbers. Given two fuzzy numbers $\tilde{A}$ and $\tilde{B}$, we say that $\tilde{A} \geq \tilde{B}$ with degree of possibility

$$v(\tilde{A} \geq \tilde{B}) = \sup_{x \geq y} \min \left(\mu_A(x), \mu_B(y) \right).$$

The symbol v, used here to denote the degree of possibility, can be interpreted as an assignment of the "truth value" to a natural language statement, or a mathematical statement. Zadeh (1978) gives the basis for the theory of possibility – the more technical discussion of the subject was given in the introduction.

Jain (1977, see also 1976, 1978) proposes another procedure. Given actions

$$h_1, h_2, \ldots, h_n$$

which have fuzzy utilities

$$\tilde{U}_1, \tilde{U}_2, \ldots, \tilde{U}_n$$

assigned to them, we rank them using the following steps:

(i) Define $r_0 = \sup\left\{r \in \mathbf{R} \colon \mu_{U_j}(r) > 0 \text{ for some } j\right\}$.

(ii) Let

$$\mu_M(x) = \left(\frac{x}{r_0}\right)^p,$$

where p is a certain parameter. We thus obtain a fuzzy set

$$\tilde{M} = (\mathbf{R}, \mu_M).$$

(iii) To each h_j assign

$$k_j = \sup\{\min\left(\mu_{U_j}(x), \mu_M(x)\right) : x \le r_0\}.$$

(iv) Rank h_j's according to their corresponding values of k_j's.

Other procedures for ranking fuzzy alternatives are also investigated by Baas and Kwakernaak (1977), Watson, Weiss, and Donnell (1979), and Buckley (1984, 1985).

A reader interested in applications of fuzzy sets in economics would be well advised to consult the work of Ponsard (1988), and also Buckley (1989, 1990, 1991), Chang (1977), Chen, Lee, and Yu (1983).

Applications of fuzzy sets in operations research can be found in its various areas, such as: decision theory (Adamo, 1980, Bellman and Zadeh, 1970, Borisov and Krumberg, 1983, Buckley, 1985 and 1990, Capocelli and De Luca, 1973, Chanas and Kambrowski, 1981, Driankov, 1987, Jain, 1976, 1977, and 1978, Kickert, 1979, Nowakowska, 1979, Yager and Basson, 1975, Yager, 1977, Zimmerman, 1987), game theory (Aubin, 1981, Butnariu, 1978 and 1980), linear programming (Buckley, 1988, 1989), control theory (Sugeno, 1985 and 1985). Zimmerman (1991) devotes Chapter 12 of his book to decision making in a fuzzy environment, and Chapter 13 to fuzzy set models in operations research.

Chapter 3: TIME VALUE OF MONEY

In his discussion of the time value of money, Trowbridge (1989) puts it very well: "The inexperienced actuary may tend to take an assumption about the time value of money as a given, and devote little or no attention to the appropriateness of the interest rate assumed. As he gains knowledge and experience, however, the actuary learns to differentiate between gross interest and net, before and after tax, nominal, effective, and real rates of interest, and internal rate of return. He gains a knowledge of the yield curve, the relationship between interest rates for different maturity periods. He recognizes that any specific interest rate has a basic component for time preference, and additional components for the possibility of default and the expectation of inflation. He knows that interest rate changes can affect assets and liabilities differently."

Yet another statement of actuarial principles brings about the inherent vagueness of certain considerations of financial natures. Dicke *et al.* (1991) write "Actuaries are often called upon to place a value on future contingent cash flows related to the operations of a financial security system. Because the actuarial value is, in general, a random variable, it may be preferable to state the conditions under which the actuarial value may be expected to fall within a given range."

Classical actuarial science (Bowers, Gerber, Hickman, Jones, and Nesbitt, 1986) considers a fixed rate of interest used for discounting future cash flows throughout the contract. Any deviations from the model are handled through the adjustment process, and conservative assumptions are used to prevent excessive risks due to such deviations. Recent volatility of the capital markets has, however, increased interest in producing models including variable interest rates which could be applied in actuarial work. Such models have been applied with a degree of success in both individual model, and collective models of life contingencies, risk theory, and pension funding. The variety of applications shows the significance of variability of rates of return – we consider this an additional incentive to look at the alternative fuzzy models.

Three classes of stochastic processes have been used to study the rates of return process $\{R_k\}$ (where k is the index of consecutive time periods considered). They are:

(a) Autoregressive-moving average process (Pollard, 1971, Panjer and Bellhouse, 1980, 1981, and Dhaene, 1989).

(b) Independent and identically distributed random variables (Boyle, 1976, Wilkie, 1976, Waters, 1978).

(c) Moving average processes (Dufresne, 1988, 1990, Frees, 1991).

The above approaches are discussed in depth in the review of probabilistic models of the rates of return process written by Dufresne (1992). Some discussion is also given by Kellison (1991). Despite reasonable success in modeling interest rates as random in the above cited works, we believe that the fuzzy sets provide a viable alternative in studying variablity of rates used in discounting. One reason is that the process of arriving at the current level of interest rates by the capital markets is immensely complex. If one attempts to predict the level of nominal interest rates a year from now, or several years ahead, estimates of probabilistic nature can be made which could allow for a reasonable guess. But a typical life insurance firm, or a pension plan, considers a time-span of ten to forty years. As Lemaire (1990) puts it: " ... To compute insurance premiums over a 40-year span with a fixed interest rate of 4.75% (...) seems to be an exercise in futility."

The task becomes even more difficult if in addition to nominal interest rate we attempt to predict the real rate, i.e., the difference between the nominal rate prevailing in the market and the inflation rate. Not only is the prediction of the inflation rate involved here, but also we attempt to model the perception of risk in the capital markets. Furthermore, the general inflation rate may not be an appropriate measure to be used by an insurer, as what counts is the rate experienced by the insurer and by the insureds – not everyone purchases the typical basket of goods considered in the Consumer Price Index, or the Producer Price Index.

Another reason for inclusion of fuzzy sets in modeling variability of rates of return is that human perception of risk, and of capital markets trends, is an inherent ingredient of those capital markets. Fuzzy sets provide a natural modeling tool for all problems involving human perception.

We will show now how calculations involving fuzzy rates of return can be handled.

Using the Extension Principle, one can define the sum of fuzzy numbers $\tilde{A}$ and $\tilde{B}$, denoted by $\tilde{A} \oplus \tilde{B} = \tilde{C}$, with the membership function

$$\mu_C(z) = \max\left\{\min\left(\mu_A(x), \mu_B(y)\right) : x + y = z\right\}.$$

Dubois and Prade (1980) show that a sum so defined is a fuzzy number, and $\oplus$ is an associative and commutative operation.

A similar application of the Extension Principle allows for the following definition of a product $\odot$ of fuzzy numbers: $\tilde{C} = \tilde{A} \odot \tilde{B}$ if

$$\mu_C(z) = \max\left\{\min\left(\mu_A(x), \mu_B(y)\right) : xy = z\right\}.$$

The product is also commutative and associative. It is also distributive with respect to the fuzzy sum operation (Dubois and Prade, 1980). One can thus define inductively an integral power of a fuzzy number $\tilde{A}$ as

$$\tilde{A}^2 = \tilde{A} \odot \tilde{A},$$
$$\tilde{A}^3 = \tilde{A}^2 \odot \tilde{A},$$
$$\cdots,$$
$$\tilde{A}^n = \tilde{A}^{n-1} \odot \tilde{A},$$
$$\cdots,$$

Once these concepts are defined, one can proceed to study "fuzzy finance".

Buckley (1987, 1991) gave a pioneering account of applications of fuzzy sets in finance and theory of interest. Calzi (1990) discusses Buckley's models and proposes some alternatives. Lemaire (1990) calculates the net single premium for a pure endowment insurance under a scenario of fuzzy interest rate.

Assuming a \$1 face value, interest rate $\tilde{i} = (i, \mu_i(j))$, and the duration of contract of n years, the fuzzy net single premium for life aged (x) is

$$\tilde{A}_{x:\overline{n}|}^{\,1} = \frac{{}_nP_x}{(1+\tilde{i})^n},$$

where the reciprocal of the fuzzy number $(1+\tilde{i})^n$ is defined in the natural way (this results in the membership function $\mu_{A_{x:\overline{n}|}^1}$ having the same value as the corresponding $\mu_i(j)$).

The above calculation, just as all standard actuarial calculations of present values, assumes a fixed interest rate over the life of the contract. The assumption will, in a sense, materialize, as a specific interest rate will be realized. However, over the life of the contract, changes in the level of interest rates, and the shape of the yield curve, will occur. If we make an assumption about fixed i, and then "fuzzify" it to $\tilde{i}$, or, as Lemaire (1990) does, consider fuzzy $(1 + i)$, we assume, in a way, the term structure of fuzzy interest rates presented in Figure 1, where the darker area represents higher degree of membership, and white area denotes zero membership value. We know that such a flat term structure of interest rates is extremely unlikely. The yield curve is most often upward sloping. This represents, depending on the theory one subscribes to, time preference of investors, or risk premium required by long-term investors. The very nature of an insurance contract is long-term. But the nonforfeiture benefits, such as cash values and dividends, are often short-term. Reserves and surplus are calculated continuously, also acquiring certain short-term nature, or at least a degree of sensitivity to short-term volatility of interest rates. One might, therefore, consider the values of interest rates given by the prevailing, at the time of calculation, yield curve, and "fuzzify" it, to represent the uncertainty about the future, vagueness of the political mechanism influencing the rates, vague and somewhat unknown inflation risk premium, and default risk premium. This would lead to a picture of a fuzzy yield curve given in Figure 2 (again, darker area represents higher degree of membership).

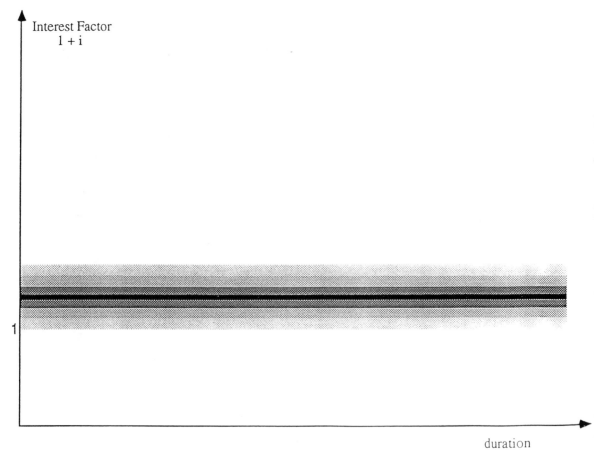

Figure 1

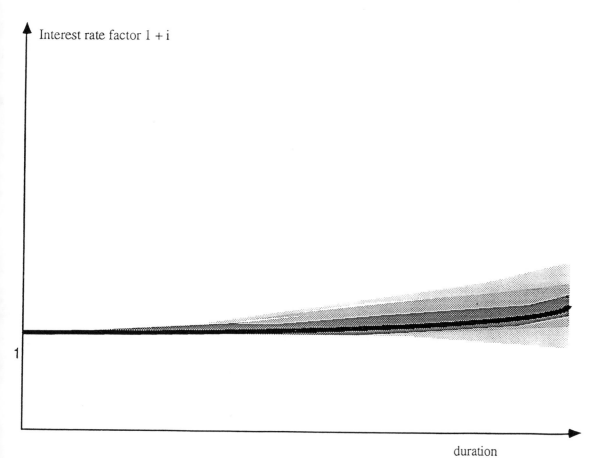

Figure 2

Lemaire (1990), in his calculation of fuzzy net single premium, models a fuzzy interest rate approximately equal to 6% as a fuzzy interest rate factor $(1 + i)$ with membership function:

$$\mu_{1+i}(x) = \begin{cases} 0 & \text{if } x \le 1.03, \\ 50x - 51.5 & \text{if } 1.03 < x \le 1.05, \\ 1 & \text{if } 1.05 < x \le 1.07, \\ 54.5 - 50x & \text{if } 1.07 < x \le 1.09, \\ 0 & \text{if } 1.09 < x. \end{cases} \tag{1}$$

We would like to propose an alternative here. It assumes current nonfuzzy short-term interest rate of 6%, with a ten-year rate being fuzzy, between 5% and 10%, and the current 10-year Treasury Note yield of 8% having membership degree of one. We can model the 10-year rate as a fuzzy number with the membership function given in Figure 3. That membership function is

$$\mu_i(j) = \begin{cases} 0 & \text{if } j \le 0.05, \\ \frac{100}{3}j - \frac{5}{3} & \text{if } 0.05 < j \le 0.08, \\ -50j + 5 & \text{if } 0.08 < j \le 0.1, \\ 0 & \text{if } 0.1 < j. \end{cases} \tag{2}$$

We assume the yield curve to be linearly rising from 6% to 8% over the duration $0 \le t \le 10$, with linearly increasing "fuzzification" of rates. The resulting fuzzy yield $\tilde{i}$ is a function of duration t, $\tilde{i}(t)$. Note that $\tilde{i}(0)$ is crisp and equals 0.06, and $\tilde{i}(10)$ is fuzzy and has the membership function given by (2). The intermediate values are determined from the linear relationship, so that $\tilde{i}(t) = \tilde{i}_t$ has the membership function:

$$\mu_{i_t}(j) = \begin{cases} 0 & \text{if } j \le 0.06 - 0.001t, \\ \frac{10}{t}\frac{100j}{3} + \left(\frac{1}{3} - \frac{20}{t}\right) & \text{if } 0.06 - 0.001t < j \le 0.06 + 0.002t, \\ -\frac{10}{t}\frac{100j}{2} + \left(2 + \frac{30}{t}\right) & \text{if } 0.06 + 0.002t < j \le 0.06 + 0.004t, \\ 0 & \text{if } 0.06 + 0.004t < j. \end{cases} \tag{3}$$

where $0 \le t \le 10$.

Lemaire (1990) calculates the net single premium for a $1,000, 10-year pure endowment policy, an a life aged (55), with $_{10}p_{55} = 0.87$ and the fuzzy interest rate of the form (1), as $\tilde{A}_{55:\overline{10}|}^{\ 1} = \tilde{A}$ with membership function:

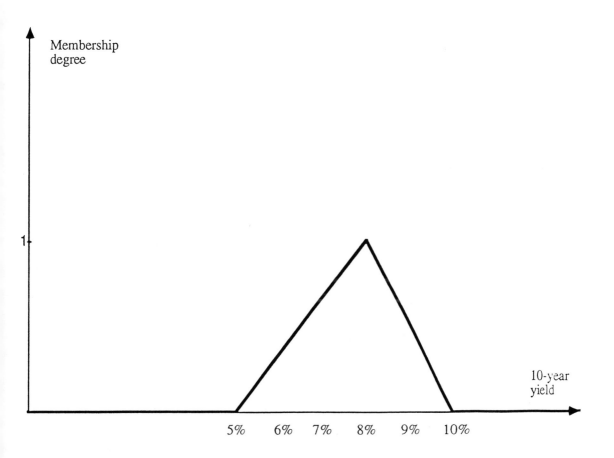

Figure 3

$$\mu_A(x) = \begin{cases} 0 & \text{if } x > \frac{870}{1.03^{10}}, \\ 50\left(\frac{870}{x}\right)^{\frac{1}{10}} - 51.5 & \text{if } \frac{870}{1.03^{10}} \geq x > \frac{870}{1.05^{10}}, \\ 1 & \text{if } \frac{870}{1.05^{10}} \geq x > \frac{870}{1.07^{10}}, \\ 54.5 - 50\left(\frac{870}{x}\right)^{\frac{1}{10}} & \text{if } \frac{870}{1.07^{10}} \geq x > \frac{870}{1.09^{10}}, \\ 0 & \text{if } \frac{870}{1.09^{10}} \geq x. \end{cases} \tag{4}$$

If we were to calculate the same net single premium under the fuzzy interest rate scenario given by (3), only the fuzzy interest rate at $t = 10$; i.e., the one given in (2) would enter into the calculation, producing a result very similar to that stated in (4), with different interest rate ranges.

Therefore it is more interesting to look at a pure term net single premium, as in this case the progressive "fuzzification" of rates with time plays a major role. To simplify our consideration, let us assume De Moivre's Law of Mortality, with $\omega = 100$, and $l_x = 100 - x$. We will consider a two-year term, \$1,000 face value, on a life aged (50), with interest rate scenario given by the formula (3). The benefit is payable at the end of the year of death. Note that the yield curve given by (3) assigns possibility of one to the two-year yield of $j = 0.06 + 0.004 = 6.4\%$. Assuming that interest rate, the net single premium calculated as a crisp number (i.e, the standard actuarial way) equals:

$$A^1_{50:\overline{2}|} = 1,000\left(vq_{50} + v^2 p_{50}q_{51}\right) \simeq 36.47.$$

Let us now consider Lemaire's model, with the fixed fuzzy two-year rate given by (3) as

$$\mu_{i_2}(j) = \begin{cases} 0 & \text{if } j \leq 0.058, \\ \frac{500}{3}j - \frac{29}{3} & \text{if } 0.058 < j \leq 0.064, \\ -250j + 17 & \text{if } 0.064 < j \leq 0.068, \\ 0 & \text{if } j > 0.068. \end{cases}$$

The net single premium (fuzzy) for this policy will then equal

$$1000\tilde{A}^1_{50:\overline{2}|} = \frac{20}{(1 + \tilde{i}_2)} \oplus \frac{20}{(1 + \tilde{i}_2)^2}.$$

Let us denote that fuzzy net single premium by $N\tilde{S}P$.

If the fuzzy number

$$\frac{20}{\left(1 + \tilde{i}_2\right)}$$

is denoted by $\tilde{M}$, it has the membership function

$$\mu_M(x) = \begin{cases} 0 & \text{if } x \geq \frac{20}{1.058} \simeq 18.90, \\ \frac{500}{3}\left(\frac{20}{x} - 1\right) - \frac{29}{3} & \text{if } \frac{20}{1.058} > x \geq \frac{20}{1.064} \simeq 18.80, \\ -250\left(\frac{20}{x} - 1\right) + 17 & \text{if } \frac{20}{1.064} > x \geq \frac{20}{1.068} \simeq 18.73, \\ 0 & \text{if } \frac{20}{1.068} > x. \end{cases}$$

and the fuzzy number

$$\frac{20}{\left(1 + \tilde{i}_2\right)^2},$$

denoted by $\tilde{N}$, has the membership function

$$\mu_N(y) = \begin{cases} 0 & \text{if } y \geq \frac{20}{(1.058)^2} \simeq 17.87, \\ \frac{500}{3}\left(\sqrt{\frac{20}{y}} - 1\right) - \frac{29}{3} & \text{if } \frac{20}{(1.058)^2} > y \geq \frac{20}{(1.064)^2} \simeq 17.67, \\ -250\left(\sqrt{\frac{20}{x}} - 1\right) + 17 & \text{if } \frac{20}{(1.064)^2} > x \geq \frac{20}{(1.068)^2} \simeq 17.53, \\ 0 & \text{if } \frac{20}{(1.068)^2} > x. \end{cases}$$

The net single premium equals $N\tilde{S}P = \tilde{M} \oplus \tilde{N}$ with the membership function

$$\mu_{NSP}(z) = \max_{x+y=z} \left(\min\left(\mu_M(x), \mu_N(y)\right)\right),$$

as defined previously. The values of $N\tilde{S}P$ for which μ_{NSP} is positive extend from 36.26 to 36.77, and the graph of the membership function of $N\tilde{S}P$ can be approximated by the one presented in Figure 4.

Now suppose that we use fully the fuzzy yield curve given by (3), with the two-year yield given by

$$\mu_{i_2}(j) = \begin{cases} 0 & \text{if } j \leq 0.058, \\ \frac{500}{3}j - \frac{29}{30} & \text{if } 0.058 < j \leq 0.064, \\ -250j + 17 & \text{if } 0.064 < j \leq 0.068, \\ 0 & \text{if } j > 0.068. \end{cases}$$

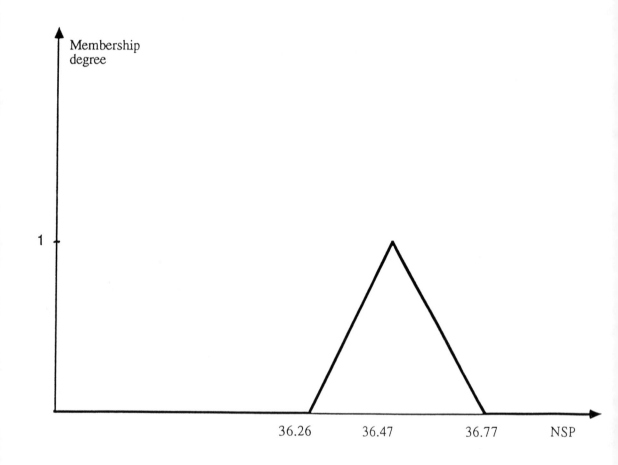

Figure 4

while the one-year yield has the membership function implied by (3):

$$\mu_{i_1}(j) = \begin{cases} 0 & \text{if } j \leq 0.059, \\ \frac{1000}{3}j - \frac{59}{3} & \text{if } 0.059 < j \leq 0.062, \\ -500j + 32 & \text{if } 0.062 < j \leq 0.064, \\ 0 & \text{if } j > 0.064. \end{cases}$$

Again, $N\tilde{S}P$ is the fuzzy net single premium, but it equals now

$$N\tilde{S}P = \frac{20}{\left(1 + \tilde{i}_1\right)} \oplus \frac{20}{\left(1 + \tilde{i}_2\right)^2}.$$

If we denote

$$\tilde{M} = \frac{20}{\left(1 + \tilde{i}_1\right)}$$

and

$$\tilde{N} = \frac{20}{\left(1 + \tilde{i}_2\right)^2},$$

we will have membership functions

$$\mu_M(x) = \begin{cases} 0 & \text{if } x \geq \frac{20}{1.059} \simeq 18.89, \\ \frac{1000}{3}\left(\frac{20}{x} - 1\right) - \frac{59}{3} & \text{if } \frac{20}{1.059} > x \geq \frac{20}{1.062} \simeq 18.83, \\ -500\left(\frac{20}{x} - 1\right) + 32 & \text{if } \frac{20}{1.062} > x \geq \frac{20}{1.064} \simeq 18.80, \\ 0 & \text{if } \frac{20}{1.064} > x \end{cases}$$

and

$$\mu_N(y) = \begin{cases} 0 & \text{if } y \geq \frac{20}{(1.058)^2} \simeq 17.87, \\ \frac{500}{3}\left(\sqrt{\frac{20}{y}} - 1\right) - \frac{29}{3} & \text{if } \frac{20}{(1.058)^2} > y \geq \frac{20}{(1.064)^2} \simeq 17.67, \\ -250\left(\sqrt{\frac{20}{x}} - 1\right) + 17 & \text{if } \frac{20}{(1.064)^2} > x \geq \frac{20}{(1.068)^2} \simeq 17.53, \\ 0 & \text{if } \frac{20}{(1.068)^2} > x. \end{cases}$$

Again

$$\mu_{NSP}(z) = \max_{x+y=z} \min\left(\mu_M(x), \mu_N(y)\right),$$

producing a membership function approximated in Figure 5.

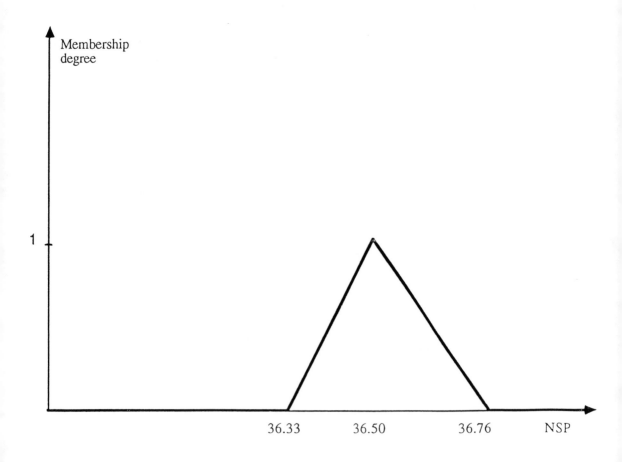

Figure 5

Chapter 4: INDIVIDUAL MODEL

In Chapter 3 we already gave examples of calculations of fuzzy actuarial functions (net single premiums) involving an individual model from the theory of life contingencies. We will now have a second look at those calculation, from a more practical perspective. As we could see at the end of Chapter 3, simple arithmetic operations get somewhat complicated in the case of fuzzy numbers. In applications, calculations such as those considered in Chapter 3, although involved, can be handled by a computer. What we need, however, is an algorithm that would simplify the model itself. With this problem in mind, we will now introduce more efficient computation formulas for fuzzy numbers, due to Dubois and Prade (1978, 1979, and 1980 Section II.2.B.e).

A *reference function* of fuzzy numbers is a function $f: \mathbf{R} \to \mathbf{R}$ such that

(i) $f(x) = f(-x)$ for $x \in \mathbf{R}$;

(ii) $f(0) = 1$;

(iii) f is nonincreasing on $[0, +\infty)$.

It is not assumed that a reference function must be differentiable, or even continuous. For example,

$$f(x) = \begin{cases} 1 & \text{if } -1 \le x \le 1, \\ 0 & \text{otherwise.} \end{cases}$$

is a reference function. On the other hand, $f(x) = e^{-x^2}$ is an example of a continuous differentiable reference function. In applications, such nicely behaved reference functions are most useful.

A fuzzy number $\tilde{M}$ is said to be an *L-R (left-right) type fuzzy number* if

$$\mu_M(x) = \begin{cases} L\left(\frac{m-x}{\alpha}\right) & \text{if } x \le m, \\ R\left(\frac{x-m}{\beta}\right) & \text{if } x \ge m, \end{cases}$$

for some reference functions L, R, and parameters $m \in \mathbf{R}$, $\alpha > 0$, $\beta > 0$. The number m is called the *mean value* of $\tilde{M}$, while α and β are called the *right* and *left* *spread*, respectively. We write often

$$\tilde{M} = (m, \alpha, \beta)_{LR}.$$

L-R type fuzzy numbers are the simplest ones to visualize, and they are the most commonly used ones. Fortunately, their form allows for a useful formula for addition of fuzzy numbers.

Theorem. (Dubois and Prade, 1978 and 1980, Section II.2.B.e.β) *If L, R, L', R' are one-to-one continuous functions on $[0, +\infty)$, and $\tilde{M} = (m, \alpha, \beta)_{LR}$ and $\tilde{N} = (n, \gamma, \delta)_{L'R'}$ are L-R type fuzzy numbers then*

$$\tilde{M} \oplus \tilde{N} = (m + n, 1, 1)_{L''R''},$$

where

$$L'' = \left(\alpha L^{-1} + \gamma (L')^{-1}\right)^{-1},$$

$$R'' = \left(\beta R^{-1} + \delta (R')^{-1}\right)^{-1},$$

with the inverses of the reference functions defined on $[0, +\infty)$.

For the interested reader, the proof of the theorem is given in the Appendix to this Chapter. The proof gives valuable insight into the L-R type fuzzy numbers.

Let us now return to calculations involving the fuzzy yield curve (3)

$$\mu_{i_t}(j) = \begin{cases} 0 & \text{if } j \leq 0.06 - 0.001t, \\ \frac{10}{t}\frac{100j}{3} + \left(\frac{1}{3} - \frac{20}{t}\right) & \text{if } 0.06 - 0.001t < j \leq 0.06 + 0.002t, \\ -\frac{10}{t}\frac{100j}{2} + \left(2 + \frac{30}{t}\right) & \text{if } 0.06 + 0.002t < j \leq 0.06 + 0.004t, \\ 0 & \text{if } 0.06 + 0.004t < j. \end{cases} \quad (3)$$

In Chapter 3 we calculated $1000\tilde{A}^1_{50:\overline{2}|}$ (assuming de Moivre's Law of mortality) only approximately. The calculation can be made more precise if the Dubois-Prade formula simplifying fuzzy addition is available.

If we use fixed fuzzy two-year interest rate $\tilde{i}_2$ as given by (3) then, as stated in Chapter 3,

$$1000\tilde{A}^1_{50:\overline{2}|} = \tilde{M} \oplus \tilde{N}$$

where

$$\tilde{M} = \frac{20}{\left(1 + \tilde{i}_2\right)}$$

and

$$\tilde{N} = \frac{20}{\left(1 + \tilde{i}_2\right)^2}.$$

These are L-R type fuzzy numbers, with, for example, the left reference function of $\tilde{M}$, say the reference function L, of the form:

$$L(w) = \frac{1064}{6 - 3.192w} - \frac{529}{3}.$$

Unfortunately, the L-R type numbers, although simple conceptually, get somewhat complicated in calculations. Of course the calculations can be easily handled by a computer, once the algorithm is defined.

Dubois and Prade (1978, 1980) also derive the following exact formulas for L-R type fuzzy numbers:

$$(m, \alpha, \beta)_{LR} \oplus (n, \gamma, \delta)_{LR} = (m + n, \alpha + \gamma, \beta + \delta)_{LR},$$

$$(m, \alpha, \beta)_{LR} \ominus (n, \gamma, \delta)_{LR} = (m - n, \alpha + \delta, \beta + \gamma)_{LR},$$

and the following approximate formulas:

$$(m, \alpha, \beta)_{LR} \odot (n, \gamma, \delta)_{LR} \simeq (mn, m\gamma + n\alpha, m\delta + n\beta)_{LR}$$

$$(\text{for } \tilde{M} > 0, \tilde{N} > 0),$$

$$(m, \alpha, \beta)_{LR} \odot (n, \gamma, \delta)_{LR} \simeq (mn, n\alpha - m\beta, n\beta - m\gamma)_{RL}$$

$$(\text{for } \tilde{M} < 0, \tilde{N} > 0),$$

$$(m, \alpha, \beta)_{LR} \odot (n, \gamma, \delta)_{LR} \simeq (mn, -n\beta - m\delta, -n\alpha - m\gamma)_{RL}$$

$$(\text{for } \tilde{M} < 0, \tilde{N} < 0).$$

The case when $\tilde{M} > 0$ and $\tilde{N} > 0$ is handled the same way as $\tilde{M} < 0$ and $\tilde{N} < 0$, as multiplication is commutative. Recall that the original definition of multiplication $\odot$ of fuzzy numbers is given by the Extension Principle in Chapter 3.

Once the formulas for fast calculations of fuzzy sums and products are available, one can extend the classical actuarial concepts of net single premium, level premium, reserve, surplus, or, in general, actuarial present value, by defining their fuzzy analogues and calculating those fuzzy analogues numerically.

One area where we think fuzzy calculations may be especially useful is calculation of future reserves. This is normally done by calculating expected future reserves (i.e., using classical probabilistic methods). When fuzzy interest rates are used, we can calculate future fuzzy reserves at a specified time first prospectively, and then retrospectively, arriving at two fuzzy numbers, which can be compared using the methods described in Chapter 2. Such calculation may reveal undesirable characteristics of current premium payment schedules and allow the company to correct them in advance.

One can also compute a fuzzy reserve prospectively at any specified time during the policy duration, once the policy has been in force until that time. This could give alternatives to the standard adjustment process. For example, for a whole life insurance of \$1 on a life originally aged (30), now aged (50), with net level annual premium of $P_{30} = A_{30}/\ddot{a}_{30}$, calculated originally as a crisp number, with a flat fuzzy yield curve $\tilde{i}$,

$$
\mu_i(j) = \begin{cases} 0 & \text{if } j \leq 0.02, \\ \frac{100}{3}j - \frac{2}{3} & \text{if } 0.02 < j \leq 0.05, \\ 1 & \text{if } 0.05 < j \leq 0.07, \\ -\frac{100}{3}j + \frac{10}{3} & \text{if } 0.07 < j \leq 0.10, \\ 0 & \text{if } j > 0.10, \end{cases}
$$

if de Moivre Law with $\omega = 70$ is assumed

$$
{}_{20}\tilde{V}_{30} = \tilde{A}_{50} \ominus P_{30}\ddot{\tilde{a}}_{50}
$$

$$
= \tilde{A}_{50} \ominus P_{30}\left(\frac{1 - \tilde{A}_{50}}{\tilde{d}}\right)
$$

$$
= \left(\bigoplus_{k=0}^{20} \frac{0.05}{(1+\tilde{i})^{k+1}}\right) \odot \left(1 + \frac{P_{30}}{\tilde{d}}\right) \ominus \frac{P_{30}}{\tilde{d}}.
$$

Numerical calculations can be now performed using the L-R type of $\tilde{i}$.

APPENDIX: Proof of Dubois and Prade's Theorem.

Recall that

$$\mu_{M \oplus N}(z) = \max_{x+y=z} \min\left(\mu_M(x), \mu_N(y)\right).$$

Note that as $\mu_M(m) = 1$ and $\mu_N(n) = 1$, we must have $\mu_{M \oplus N}(m+n) = 1$, as one is the overall maximum value that $\min\left(\mu_M(x), \mu_N(y)\right)$ can attain. Observe also that if $x + y = z < m + n$ with $x < m$ and $y > n$ then there is a $y' < n$ such that $\mu_N(y') \geq \mu_N(y)$ and x' such that $x < x' < m$ and $x' + y' = z$ (observe that $\mu_M(x') \geq \mu_M(x)$ by definition of μ_M. Therefore for $z < m + n$ we can calculate $\mu_{M \oplus N}(z)$ as

$$\max\left\{\min\left(\mu_M(x), \mu_N(y)\right) : x \leq m, y \leq n, x + y = z\right\}.$$

Similarly, for $z > m + n$

$$\mu_{M \oplus N}(z) = \max\left\{\min\left(\mu_M(x), \mu_N(y)\right) : x \geq m, y \geq n, x + y = z\right\}.$$

If $z' < z'' < m + n$ then for any x', y' such that $x' + y' = z'$ we can choose $x'' > x'$, $y'' > y'$ with $x'' < m$, $y'' < n$ and $\mu_M(x'') > \mu_M(x')$, $\mu_N(y'') > \mu_N(y')$ so that

$$\mu_{M \oplus N}(z'') > \mu_{M \oplus N}(z')$$

which implies that $\tilde{M} \oplus \tilde{N}$ is an L-R type fuzzy number (as the proof of the appropriate inequality for $z > m + n$ is analogous).

For $x \leq m$,

$$\alpha L^{-1}\left(\mu_M(x)\right) = m - x,$$

$$\gamma \left(L'\right)^{-1}\left(\mu_N(y)\right) = n - y,$$

so that, if $z = x + y$,

$$(m + n) - (x + y) = (m + n) - z = \alpha L^{-1}\left(\mu_M(x)\right) + \gamma \left(L'\right)^{-1}\left(\mu_N(y)\right).$$

It is now enough to note the fact that continuity of L and L' allows us to assume that for some x and y, $\mu_M(x) = \mu_N(y)$ and exactly that pair produces the maximum value of $\min\left(\mu_M(x), \mu_N(y)\right)$ – if $\mu_M(x)$ rises, $\mu_N(y)$ must fall so that the minimum falls, while if $\mu_M(x)$ falls, the same result is produced, despite the fact that $\mu_N(y)$ rises, as the minimum of the two values is considered.

Chapter 5: COLLECTIVE MODELS

Before we proceed to discuss opportunities for introduction of fuzzy sets in the study of collective models, we would like to make another reference to the unique monograph of Smithson (1989). In Section 2.2, Smithson discusses two traditional normative pragmatisms – in structural engineering and jurisprudence. The importance of the two lies in the severity of failure when dealing with uncertainty in either of the practices. As Smithson puts it "... let us consider what these two professional spheres have in common. One shared feature is an overriding conservatism toward speculation and trial-and-error method of inquiry. Unlike the scientist (or at least a Popperian), neither the judge nor the structural engineer wish their operational rules and procedures to be falsified. They are interested in avoiding failure, and maximizing certainty or knowledge is merely one strategy among many for accomplishing this goal." One can only wonder why actuaries are not listed as the third group of professionals with those characteristics! When building individual models, an actuary proceeds in a manner similar to that of a mathematician – constructing a theoretical model. But collective models are those directly applied in practice, and failure becomes very costly when it happens to the insurer – after all, the insureds enter into contracts precisely to avoid risk of failure. Smithson points out that "Traditional engineering criteria and rules for ensuring structural safety in the absense of empirical tests are based on two related strategies. The first is to estimate a 'worst case' load (or stress) scenario and apply it to theoretical computations of the capacity of the proposed structure, and the second is to use safety factors to ensure that the 'worst case' calculations exceed the likely actual loads and stresses by an appropriate margin of safety." The two sound very much like simulations of surplus level under the worst case scenario, and adding the security loading to the premium charged. In either case, one can model the 'worst case' scenario, or the security loading, as fuzzy, thus giving a better perspective on the possibility of failure.

There are three specific areas where we believe some benefit can be gained by considering fuzzy set-theoretic models in collective arrangements.

44

In the area of defined benefit pension plans, one of the actuary's roles is that of arriving at the appropriate actuarial discount rate in funding calculations. Although adjustments to that rate are possible, and practiced periodically, one can certainly envision a situation when an adjustment results in an increase of the Projected Benefit Obligation, while the company finds itself in a precarious position of not being able to increase the funding of the plan. Alternatively, the obligations could be lowered at the time when the company is most able to increase contributions (not an unusual scenario in the 1980's for companies whose pension plans had significant equity markets exposure), sometimes even resulting in an overfunding, viewed as an opportunity in the case of a takeover or a leveraged buyout. The problem with such an opportunity is of course that the second of the situations described above is usually followed by the first.

We suggest a possibility of presenting a "possibility distribution" of interest rates, or simply a fuzzy interest rate – that is a certain range of possible discount rates, in the actuary's report to the management, with each interest rate, and the corresponding Projected Benefit Obligation and Accumulated Benefit Obligation, assigned its membership value between zero and one. This may be presented as a supplement to the actuary's standard calculation, or even a footnote to the annual report of a company, resulting in a consideration of the entire range of possible interest rates when viewing an apparently overfunded (or underfunded) pension plan.

The second area where there may be some distinct value in applying fuzzy set methods is that of short-term group model. A group is, as Trowbridge puts it, "a continuously changing collection of covered individuals." Even though the initial premiums are set after considering averages of rates and claims of classifications covered within the group, those classifications change dynamically. Therefore one can envision setting the weights of classifications as fuzzy numbers, due to their unstable nature, allowing for possibilities of future changes, and more conservatism in the derivation of the premium.

One can also notice a somewhat "fuzzy" approach of similar nature in the fundamental model of the credibility theory. The credibility factor Z assigned to claim parameter f_2 of a newly observed subsection may be viewed not only as a random variable, but alternatively as a measure of possibility of f_2, while $1 - Z$ measures the possibility of the best a priori estimate of a claim parameter.

The final possibility of applications of fuzzy set theory in collective models which we see now is in the Social Insurance Model. The United States Social Security System, and similar social insurance schemes in other countries, are systems which must balance projections of disbursements over a very long time period, and projections of income over the same period, with respect to current participants, future participansts, and their dependents. Not only the system is immensely complicated, it is also subject to political interpretations and perceptions.

In the United States, actuarial reports to Congress are presented with four possible scenarios of the future changes in the economy, interest rates, and other factors influencing the system. One of the scenarios is called "optimistic", one "pessimistic", and the other two are intermediate (Andrews and Beekman, 1987). Invariably, political decision makers, acting in their rational political self-interest, pick the scenario which is beneficial to their agenda, as the most likely. But the possibility weights should not be assigned to the scenarios by their end-users, but rather by their creators, or by economists. Those possibility weights do not have to be probabilities, but rather can express perception of the experts of subjective likelihood (i.e., fuzzy possibility) of the scenario. An "optimistic" scenario which is given with only 25% possibility weight would be more difficult to pick than an 80% certain recession prognosis. In fact, the report could even expand the number of scenarios, and give one general fuzzy scenario.

Chapter 6: CLASSIFICATION

This topic is one of the most controversial in today's insurance industry, as it is entangled in numerous political issues. Trowbridge (1989) provides a simple argument showing that when facing a two-group market, with one group of significantly higher risk, uniform pricing by the insurer results in antiselection; i.e., providing a disproportionate share of coverage to the high-risk group, while losing the business of the low-risk group.

The main reason why classification gives rise to controversy is the fact that it is often, correctly or not, viewed as economic *price discrimination*. Stigler (1987) defines: "... price discrimination is present when two or more similar goods are sold at prices that are in different ratio to marginal cost." Note that the excess of price over marginal cost represents the economic profit (i.e., profit after considering accounting costs, *and* opportunity cost, including the cost of capital). Only firms acting as monopolies, or with significant market power, can price discriminate. As Varian (1989) puts it: "For to say that price is in excess of marginal cost is to say that there is someone who is willing to pay more than the cost of production for an extra unit of the good. Lowering the price for all consumers may well be unprofitable, but lowering the price to the marginal consumer alone will likely be profitable."

Even with significant competition in the insurance marketplace, firms do seem to have market power. Entry into the industry is limited, not only due to regulatory constraints, but capital requirements, and the surplus strain endangering a newly established insurer. Furthermore, personal arbitrage among the consumers is not possible in insurance. This would suggest the industry is well fit for price discrimination practices, at least theoretically. Stiglitz (1977) gives a view of price discrimination in insurance.

Pigou (1920) gave the traditional classification of the forms of price discrimination. *First degree* (or *perfect*) price discrimination occurs when the seller is able to charge for each unit of the good the highest price at which consumer is still willing

47

to buy it (*the reservation price*). An auction is a practical model of this form of discrimination.

Second-degree price discrimination, also called *nonlinear pricing*, occurs when prices differ depending on the number of units of the good bought, but not across the consumers. Here coupons, or quantity discounts, are obvious examples.

Third-degree price discrimination means that the entire market is segmented by the seller into homogeneous, and separated, submarkets, each of which is charged its own profit-maximizing price.

As Varian (1989) puts it "Price discrimination has long been regarded as a dubious practice from the legal viewpoint, though the complaints about the practice voiced by legislators are typically not those voiced by economists." Indeed, price discrimination is the topic of major pieces of antitrust legislation. The Clayton Act of 1914 (Section 2) states "That it shall be unlawful for any person engaged in commerce ... to discriminate in price between different purchasers of commodities ... where the effect of such discrimination may be to substantially lessen competition or tend to create monopoly in any line of commerce;", but the statement is followed by rather general exclusions. The intent of the law was apparently to protect small businesses from being "undercut" in certain regions by large competitors, not to protect the end consumer. The Robinson-Patman Act of 1936 strengthened the prohibition of price discrimination to all cases when it "directly or indirectly ... lessen(s) competition or tend(s) to create a monopoly in any line of commerce, or to injure, destroy, or prevent competition..."

Even though the McCarran-Ferguson Act (see Lazarescu and Philips, 1992) exempts from the antitrust laws the "business of insurance" to the extent that states regulate those activities, the "business of insurance" is understood to be limited to spreading of insurance risk and to insurance companies' relationship with their policyholders. Moreover, the existence of the Clayton Act and the Robinson-Patman act creates a political atmosphere where an accusation of price discrimination is viewed as a serious one. We have witnessed numerous attempts to legislate unisex life insurance pricing, despite the significant body of evidence pointing towards

48

longer life expectancy for women in the twentieth century.

This is an especially sensitive issue when insurance itself is mandated by legislation, or some government regulation. As Trowbridge (1989) points out, mandatory car insurance for inner city inhabitants who are automatically considered higher risk is not, and cannot be, viewed favorably by them.

Yet there is a mounting economic evidence that price discrimination may lead to more efficient allocation of resources. Furthermore, the review of the study of price discrimination in insurance by Stiglitz (1977) suggests that perception of classification as discrimination is erroneous, and lack of classification may in fact lead to discrimination in the economic sense of the word.

Let us review the basic results of Stiglitz (1977). They refer only to casualty insurance, no time value of money enters into consideration, and two groups of consumers exist: low risk and high risk. Yet the model, however simplified, provides a significant insight into the economics of insurance. The major property of the equilibrium pricing is that the *two groups of consumers (i.e., different risks) never purchase the same contract.* Under perfect competition with perfect information, two groups have two separate complete insurance policies at actuarial odds. Under perfect competition with imperfect information, the high-risk group purchases complete insurance at actuarial odds, and the low-risk group buys partial insurance at actuarial odds. With monopoly pricing (or at least some degree of market power) and perfect information, high-risk group purchases complete insurance at terms which make an individual indifferent to buying no insurance, and the low-risk group also purchases complete insurance at terms which make an individual indifferent to buying no insurance. Under imperfect information and monopoly, however, the high-risk individuals purchase complete insurance at terms which range from those which make a high-risk individual indifferent to buying insurance to terms which make a low-risk individual indifferent to buying insurance. It should be added that in this scenario, insurance firms may be forced to accept a loss on a contract. The low-risk individuals purchase partial or no insurance; terms are always such as to make an individual indifferent to buying no insurance.

49

The above overview of Stiglitz's results clearly indicates that, from the economic standpoint, *classification of risks is not price discrimination*. In fact, it is lack of classification that proves itself to be an economic equivalent of discrimination.

In view of the above, the efforts put forth by actuaries in order to improve classification methods, are highly commendable.

In this chapter, we would like to point out two areas where fuzzy sets could be of assistance in improving classification.

The politically controversial forms of classification are based on criteria of some social importance. In life insurance, distinguishing between men and women may be viewed as a derivative of practices of sex discrimination in the workplace. In casualty insurance, car insurance rates based on one's place of residence may be viewed as directed against inner city inhabitants, and alleged to be racially motivated. It is difficult and costly from the standpoint of public relations, to deal with such accusations. What we would like to point out here is that a possible precaution against such difficult situations is to create classification methods with no assumptions, but rather methods which *discover patterns* used in classification.

One can view experience adjustments, and classification based on experience, as such a form of classification of risk – based solely on data, not on preconceived perception of risk. Note that Hallin (1977), Hallin and Inglebleek (1981), and Van Eeghen, Greup and Nijssen (1983) apply statistical methods to create a procedure of rate making based solely on available data. We will suggest here a fuzzy alternative.

One of the new dynamic fields of modern applied mathematics is that of *pattern recognition*. Bezdek (1981) defines pattern recognition simply as "A search for structure in data." Generally speaking, the task is to divide n objects, where n is a positive integer, $x_1, x_2, \ldots, x_n$, which are characterized by p of their indicators, into c, $2 \leq c < n$ categorically homogeneous subsets which are called *clusters*. The objects belonging to the same cluster should be similar and the objects in different clusters should be as dissimilar as possible. The number of clusters, c, is normally known in advance.

The most important question which has to be answered before applying any clustering procedure is: which properties of the data set that can be described mathematically should be used, and in which way should they be used in order to identify clusters.

In the case of risk classification, the purpose is, of course, distinguishing between risks that are significantly different. There is always the question of how the costs of classifications compare to savings brought by improvements in the classification process, but this question is beyond the scope of this work. We will, instead, concentrate on the second natural question: given an accepted pattern of division of risks, to what degree is it a product of tradition, and to what degree is it justified by real differences? Statistical significance may not be sufficient. A population consisting of 90% high-risk individuals and 10% low-risk individuals will be significantly different from that with 10% high-risk individuals and 90% low-risk individuals. But then there is a more efficient way to partition the union of the two populations according to risk.

We believe that clustering methods can be used to produce more efficient methods of classification. The topic requires, most likely, further research, especially of an empirical nature, but the basic theoretical ideas are presented and illustrated here.

Classical clustering algorithms generate patterns such that each object is assigned to exactly one cluster. Often, however, objects cannot appropriately be assigned to strictly one cluster, because they are, in some way, "between" clusters. Fuzzy clustering methods have proved themselves to be a powerful tool for representing data structure in such a situation.

We will present the basic methods of clustering. The data set

$$X = \{\mathbf{x}_1, \mathbf{x}_2, \ldots, \mathbf{x}_n\}$$

is assumed to be a finite subset of a p-dimensional Euclidean space $\mathbf{R}^p$. Each $\mathbf{x}_k = (x_{k,1}, x_{k,2}, \ldots, x_{k,p})$, $k = 1, 2, 3, \ldots, n$ is called a *feature vector*, while each $x_{k,j}$, where $j = 1, 2, \ldots, p$, is the j-th *feature* of observation $\mathbf{x}_k$.

51

A partition of the data set X into clusters is described by the membership functions of the elements of the cluster (note that such a description could also apply to crisp clusters, with the membership function meaning simply the characteristic function). The clusters are denoted by $\tilde{S}_1, \tilde{S}_2, \ldots, \tilde{S}_c$ with the corresponding membership functions $\mu_{S_1}, \mu_{S_2}, \ldots, \mu_{S_c}$.

A $c \times n$ matrix

$$\tilde{U} = [\mu_{S_i}(\mathbf{x}_k)]_{i=1,2,\ldots,c;\, k=1,2,\ldots,n}$$

is a *fuzzy c-partition* if it satisfies the following conditions:

1. $\sum_{i=1}^{c} \mu_{S_i}(\mathbf{x}_k) = 1$ for each $k = 1, 2, \ldots, n$.

2. $0 \leq \sum_{k=1}^{n} \mu_{S_i}(\mathbf{x}_k) \leq n$ for each $i = 1, 2, \ldots, c$.

The conditions 1. and 2. have the following intuitive interpretation: 1. says that each feature vector $\mathbf{x}_k$ has its total membership of one divided among all clusters, while 2. says that the sum of membership degrees of feature vectors in a given cluster does not exceed the total number of feature vectors.

We will now describe, and illustrate by an example, an algorithm for generating fuzzy partitions, following Bezdek (1981). The idea is as follows: the initial partition will be determined by our best guess, or experience, then in each cluster we will identify its *center* $\mathbf{v}_i$, $i = 1, 2, \ldots, c$ (it is meant to be an element which captures the essential features of the cluster), and calculate the weighted sum of distances given by the vector norm of elements of clusters from the corresponding centers. We will then modify the initial partition in order to minimize that weighted sum.

Recall that p is the total number of features (coordinates of feature vectors). Let

$$G = [g_{jl}]_{1 \leq j, l \leq p}$$

be a symmetric, positive-definite, real-valued matrix. We introduce a vector norm defined by that matrix

$$\|\mathbf{x}_k - \mathbf{v}_i\|_G = \sqrt{(\mathbf{x}_k - \mathbf{v}_i)^T G (\mathbf{x}_k - \mathbf{v}_i)}$$

$$= \sqrt{\sum_{j=1}^{p} \sum_{l=1}^{p} g_{jl} (\mathbf{x}_{kj} - \mathbf{v}_{il})^2}. \tag{5}$$

Bezdek (1981) actually defines an entire family of algorithms, one for each positive parameter m. Here are the steps:

STEP 1:

Choose c, an integer between 2 and n, the number of clusters the data will be partitioned into;

Choose a positive parameter m, and a symmetric, positive-definite $p \times p$ matrix G. Define the norm $\| \ \|_G$ as in (5).

Choose the initial fuzzy partition

$$\tilde{U}^{(0)} = \left[\mu_{S_i}^{(0)}(\mathbf{x}_k) \right]_{1 \leq i \leq c, 1 \leq k \leq n}.$$

Choose a parameter $\varepsilon > 0$ (this number will tell us when to stop the iteration process).

Set the iteration counting parameter l equal to 0.

STEP 2:

Calculate the fuzzy cluster centers $\{\mathbf{v}_i^{(l)}\}_{i=1,2,\ldots,c}$ given by the following formula:

$$\mathbf{v}_i^{(l)} = \frac{\sum_{k=1}^n \left(\mu_{S_i}^{(l)}(\mathbf{x}_k) \right)^m \mathbf{x}_k}{\sum_{k=1}^n \left(\mu_{S_i}^{(l)}(\mathbf{x}_k) \right)^m}$$

for $i = 1, 2, \ldots, c$.

STEP 3:

Calculate the new partition (i.e., membership matrix)

$$\tilde{U}^{(l+1)} = \left[\mu_{S_i}^{(l+1)}(\mathbf{x}_k) \right]_{1 \leq i \leq c, 1 \leq k \leq n},$$

where

$$\mu_{S_i}^{(l+1)}(\mathbf{x}_k) = \frac{\sqrt[m-1]{\dfrac{1}{\|\mathbf{x}_k - \mathbf{v}_i^{(l)}\|_G^2}}}{\sum_{j=1}^c \sqrt[m-1]{\dfrac{1}{\|\mathbf{x}_k - \mathbf{v}_j^{(l)}\|_G^2}}} \tag{6}$$

where $i = 1, 2, \ldots, c$ and $k = 1, 2, \ldots, n$.

If $\mathbf{x}_k = \mathbf{v}_i^{(l)}$, however, the formula (6) cannot be used, and we simply set

$$\mu_{S_j}^{(l+1)}(\mathbf{x}_k) = \begin{cases} 1 & \text{if } j = i, \\ 0 & \text{if } j \neq i, \ j = 1, 2, \ldots, c. \end{cases}$$

53

STEP 4:

By using the natural matrix norm, or the extension of $\| \ \|_G$ to the matrix norm, or by choosing a different, more suitable to the problem considered, matrix norm, calculate

$$\Delta = \|\tilde{U}^{(l+1)} - \tilde{U}^{(l)}\|_G.$$

If $\Delta > \varepsilon$, repeat all steps. Otherwise stop.

Before we proceed to illustrate the algorithm with an actuarial example, let us note the importance of the parameter m. It is called the *exponential weight*. Its purpose is to reduce the influence of "noise" in data – m reduces the influence of small values of membership functions for data points and increases the role of the larger values of the membership functions. The larger m is, the stronger its influence. For a discussion of its significance, consult Windham (1982, p. 358), also Bezdek (1981).

It should be also added that Bock (1979) and Bezdek (1981) discuss and prove convergence of the algorithm presented here.

We will now provide an example of how this algorithm could be of value to an actuary. Consider a population consisting of four persons:

Person 1 – age: 30, height: 175 cm, gender: male (written as 0), weight: 92 kG, resting pulse: 110;

Person 2 – age: 30, height: 185 cm, gender: male (written as 0), weight: 75 kG, resting pulse: 70;

Person 3 – age: 30, height: 160 cm, gender: female (written as 1), weight: 55 kG, resting pulse: 72;

Person 4 – age: 30, height: 150 cm, gender: female (written as 1), weight: 90 kG, resting pulse: 100.

We will represent these persons by four feature vectors with four coordinates (age is the same for all of them, so it is not included as a feature):

$$\mathbf{x}_1 = \begin{bmatrix} 175.0 \\ 0.0 \\ 92.0 \\ 110.0 \end{bmatrix}, \ \mathbf{x}_2 = \begin{bmatrix} 185.0 \\ 0.0 \\ 75.0 \\ 70.0 \end{bmatrix}, \ \mathbf{x}_3 = \begin{bmatrix} 160.0 \\ 1.0 \\ 55.0 \\ 72.0 \end{bmatrix}, \ \mathbf{x}_4 = \begin{bmatrix} 150.0 \\ 1.0 \\ 90.0 \\ 100.0 \end{bmatrix}.$$

We will seek two fuzzy clusters among these four feature vectors (i.e., $c = 2$). In order to balance the influences of the four factors, we will choose the matrix

$$
G = \begin{bmatrix} 0.001 & 0 & 0 & 0 \\ 0 & 1.0 & 0 & 0 \\ 0 & 0 & 0.0025 & 0 \\ 0 & 0 & 0 & 0.0025 \end{bmatrix}
$$

to be the one determining the norm $\| \; \|_G$. This choice is rather arbitrary and a better one can be determined through studying experience – most notably, the norm above will not account for any interactive effect.

We will let $m = 2$, and set the initial partition as

$$
\tilde{U}^{(0)} = \begin{bmatrix} 0 & 0 & 1 & 1 \\ 1 & 1 & 0 & 0 \end{bmatrix} \tag{7}
$$

Note that the partition (7) divides the population into clusters solely on the base of gender.

We also choose $\varepsilon = \frac{1}{5}$ as the stopping rule, with the standard matrix norm being used for calculation of the distance of matrices (the standard matrix norm treats matrices as vectors in the Euclidean space with the number of coordinates equal to the number of entries of a matrix).

We start by calculating the fuzzy cluster centers $\mathbf{v}_1^{(0)}$, and $\mathbf{v}_2^{(0)}$. We have

$$
\begin{aligned}
\mathbf{v}_1^{(0)} &= \frac{\sum_{k=1}^4 \left(\mu_{S_1}^{(0)}(\mathbf{x}_k) \right)^2 \mathbf{x}_k}{\sum_{k=1}^4 \left(\mu_{S_1}^{(0)}(\mathbf{x}_k) \right)^2} \\
&= \frac{\mathbf{x}_3 + \mathbf{x}_4}{2} \\
&= \begin{bmatrix} 155.0 \\ 1.0 \\ 72.5 \\ 86.0 \end{bmatrix},
\end{aligned}
$$

and

$$
\mathbf{v}_2^{(0)} = \frac{\mathbf{x}_1 + \mathbf{x}_2}{2} = \begin{bmatrix} 180.0 \\ 0.0 \\ 83.5 \\ 90.0 \end{bmatrix}.
$$

Now we are ready to calculate the entries of the new partition matrix

$$
\tilde{U}^{(1)} = \left[\mu_{S_i}^{(1)}(\mathbf{x}_k) \right], \quad i = 1, 2, \; k = 1, 2, 3, 4.
$$

We have

$$\mu_{S_1}^{(1)}(\mathbf{x}_1) = \frac{\frac{1}{\|\mathbf{x}_1 - \mathbf{v}_1^{(0)}\|_G^2}}{\frac{1}{\|\mathbf{x}_1 - \mathbf{v}_1^{(0)}\|_G^2} + \frac{1}{\|\mathbf{x}_1 - \mathbf{v}_2^{(0)}\|_G^2}} \simeq 0.24.$$

and

$$\mu_{S_1}^{(1)}(\mathbf{x}_2) \simeq 0.32,$$

$$\mu_{S_1}^{(1)}(\mathbf{x}_3) \simeq 0.82,$$

$$\mu_{S_1}^{(1)}(\mathbf{x}_4) \simeq 0.64,$$

$$\mu_{S_2}^{(1)}(\mathbf{x}_1) \simeq 0.76,$$

$$\mu_{S_2}^{(1)}(\mathbf{x}_2) \simeq 0.68,$$

$$\mu_{S_2}^{(1)}(\mathbf{x}_3) \simeq 0.18,$$

$$\mu_{S_2}^{(1)}(\mathbf{x}_4) \simeq 0.36.$$

This results in a new partition

$$\tilde{U}^{(1)} \simeq \begin{bmatrix} 0.24 & 0.32 & 0.82 & 0.64 \\ 0.76 & 0.68 & 0.18 & 0.36 \end{bmatrix}.$$

Note that even though Person 2 is still mostly in Cluster 2, that person's feature vector is significantly closer to $\mathbf{v}_1^{(1)}$ than it is to $\mathbf{v}_1^{(0)}$. Similar observation can be made about Person 4 and Cluster 1. Of course, the initial data was intentionally designed in such a way that if it were not for the second coordinate of the feature vectors (i.e., gender), we would be very much inclined to cluster Persons 1 and 4 together, and then Persons 2 and 3 together in the second cluster.

We check the stopping procedure and get

$$\|\tilde{U}^{(0)} - \tilde{U}^{(1)}\| = \sqrt{2 \cdot 0.24^2 + 2 \cdot 0.32^2 + 2 \cdot 0.18^2 + 2 \cdot 0.36^2} =$$

$$= \sqrt{0.644} = 0.8024961 > \varepsilon.$$

We need to proceed with the next iteration of the algorithm. The new centers of the fuzzy clusters are:

$$\mathbf{v}_1^{(1)} \simeq \begin{bmatrix} 159.46 \\ 0.87 \\ 69.91 \\ 82.83 \end{bmatrix}$$

and

$$\mathbf{v}_2^{(1)} \simeq \begin{bmatrix} 175.75 \\ 0.13 \\ 84.25 \\ 92.51 \end{bmatrix}.$$

Now

$$\|\mathbf{x}_1 - \mathbf{v}_1^{(1)}\|_G = 2.0158954 \simeq 2.02.$$

Similarly we calculate

$$\|\mathbf{x}_1 - \mathbf{v}_2^{(1)}\|_G \simeq 0.97,$$

$$\|\mathbf{x}_2 - \mathbf{v}_1^{(1)}\|_G \simeq 1.37,$$

$$\|\mathbf{x}_2 - \mathbf{v}_2^{(1)}\|_G \simeq 1.26,$$

$$\|\mathbf{x}_3 - \mathbf{v}_1^{(1)}\|_G \simeq 1.27,$$

$$\|\mathbf{x}_3 - \mathbf{v}_2^{(1)}\|_G \simeq 2.05,$$

$$\|\mathbf{x}_4 - \mathbf{v}_1^{(1)}\|_G \simeq 1.36,$$

$$\|\mathbf{x}_4 - \mathbf{v}_2^{(1)}\|_G \simeq 1.28.$$

Based on the above, we obtain

$$\tilde{U}^{(2)} \simeq \begin{bmatrix} 0.32 & 0.48 & 0.62 & 0.48 \\ 0.68 & 0.52 & 0.38 & 0.52 \end{bmatrix}.$$

The stopping test gives

$$\|\tilde{U}^{(1)} - \tilde{U}^{(2)}\| = 0.4418144 > \varepsilon.$$

Yet another iteration is needed. We proceed to calculate the new cluster centers

$$\mathbf{v}_1^{(2)} \simeq \begin{bmatrix} 165.27 \\ 0.65 \\ 72.37 \\ 82.43 \end{bmatrix}$$

and

$$\mathbf{v}_2^{(2)} \simeq \begin{bmatrix} 169.58 \\ 0.36 \\ 82.87 \\ 93.44 \end{bmatrix}.$$

This gives

$$\|\mathbf{x}_1 - \mathbf{v}_1^{(2)}\|_G \simeq 1.84,$$

$$\|\mathbf{x}_1 - \mathbf{v}_2^{(2)}\|_G \simeq 1.03,$$

$$\|\mathbf{x}_2 - \mathbf{v}_1^{(2)}\|_G \simeq 1.10,$$

$$\|\mathbf{x}_2 - \mathbf{v}_2^{(2)}\|_G \simeq 1.38,$$

$$\|\mathbf{x}_3 - \mathbf{v}_1^{(2)}\|_G \simeq 1.08,$$

$$\|\mathbf{x}_3 - \mathbf{v}_2^{(2)}\|_G \simeq 1.90,$$

$$\|\mathbf{x}_4 - \mathbf{v}_1^{(2)}\|_G \simeq 1.38,$$

$$\|\mathbf{x}_4 - \mathbf{v}_2^{(2)}\|_G \simeq 1.01.$$

The resulting new fuzzy partition matrix is

$$\tilde{U}^{(3)} \simeq \begin{bmatrix} 0.36 & 0.56 & 0.64 & 0.42 \\ 0.64 & 0.44 & 0.36 & 0.58 \end{bmatrix}.$$

We now have

$$\|\tilde{U}^{(2)} - \tilde{U}^{(3)}\| = 0.1549193 < \varepsilon = \frac{1}{5}.$$

The algorithm stops here. $\tilde{U}^{(3)}$ is the final partition matrix. It is most natural to use the degree of membership of more than 0.5 (i.e, use 0.5-cuts) as the criterion for determining where the dividing line of classification should be drawn. Note that we started by putting $\mathbf{x}_1$ and $\mathbf{x}_2$ into one cluster, and $\mathbf{x}_3$ and $\mathbf{x}_4$ into the other, but we finish with $\mathbf{x}_2$ and $\mathbf{x}_3$ being in one cluster, and $\mathbf{x}_1$ and $\mathbf{x}_4$ in the other. Thus we started by classifying risks by gender, and concluded that a more efficient classification, based on all available evidence, exists. We have, therefore, with the use of fuzzy sets, "substituted facts for appearances and demonstrations for impressions."

In the final comment on fuzzy pattern recognition, it should be stressed that the algorithm presented here, and the consequent approach to risk classification, is by no means unique. Pattern recognition is a very dynamic, rapidly developing field, and new improved algorithms, including fuzzy ones, are constantly produced. Some new ideas in this area are discussed by Kosko (1991). A reader interested in fundamental concepts may consult Chapter 11 of Zimmerman (1991).

The second main "fuzzy idea" which may be fruitful in classification is in fact the one that gives fuzzy sets theory its main claim to fame. As fuzzy sets are created to model imprecise human reasoning, and to describe processes which by their nature escape precise descriptions, fuzzy set theory should produce results which will allow for replacing humans in at least some of those imprecise human functions.

An *expert system* is, as its name says, a system built in order to replace a human expert. In the discussion of approximate reasoning in Chapter 1 we gave an example of a shopper from Chapter 1 in a grocery store thinking "This tomato is more red than the other ones. A ripe tomato is red. Therefore this tomato is more ripe than the other ones." Such thinking is not easy to model using the traditional Aristotelian/Boolean logic. And, as we stressed in Chapter 1, such reasoning is an integral part of our lives, not just during trips to grocery stores, but also in decisions commonly considered to be of much greater importance (we do not imply necessarily that such ordering of importance is true).

Lemaire (1990) gives an example of a medical statement concerning an applicant for life insurance:

"If applicant exercises regularly,

and does not smoke,

and has low level of cholesterol,

and has low blood pressure,   (8)

and has appropriate weight,

then the applicant has higher life expectancy."

Higher life expectancy implies possibility of being classified as a preferred risk. Obviously, similar medical statements can be given for high risk applicants.

Parts of the statement (8) are somewhat precise. Smoking is a 0-1 process; you either smoke or you do not. A certain numerical level of cholesterol; e.g., 200, can be set as the upper acceptable limit. Similarly, standards for exercise, blood pressure, and weight, can be established. But unlike smoking (or family history of kidney or heart disease, stroke or diabetes) the other factors are not as strict in real life experience, as they are in the insurance companies' guidelines. To quote Lemaire (1990): "Insurers demand all conditions to be strictly met; the slightest infringement leads to automatic rejection of the preferred category. (...) A cholesterol level of 200 is accepted, a level of 201 is not!"

Why are the insurers so strict? The answer is obvious if we recall Stiglitz's (1977) results about economics of insurance – bundling of different risks results in low risk individuals either purchasing only partial insurance or no insurance at all (such bundling, in fact, does not appear in any economic equilibrium situation!). In actuarial language – antiselection is the key.

However, such strict criteria may in fact have precisely the opposite effect. A wide class of individuals who are close to all, or some, boundaries, may be bundled with high risks. This creates an incentive for them to abandon the contract. As much as antiselection is a part of "insurance life", its minimization is the key to making insurance equitable, and economically sound.

Lemaire (1990) proposes the following solution to the problem of defining preferred risk more precisely – by making it fuzzy! Each prospective policyholder is represented by a data vector $\mathbf{x} = (t_1, t_2, t_3, t_4)$, where

$t_1 = $ the total level of cholesterol in the blood (in mg/dl);

$t_2 = $ the systolic blood pressure (in mm of Hg);

$t_3 = $ the ratio of the effective weight to the recommended weight, as a function of height and build;

$t_4 = $ the average consumption of cigarettes per day.

Lemaire (1990) then constructs the fuzzy set $\tilde{A}$ of people with low level of cholesterol

$$\mu_A(t_1) = \begin{cases} 1 & \text{if } t_1 \le 200, \\ 1 - 2\left(\frac{t_1 - 200}{40}\right)^2 & \text{if } 200 < t_1 \le 220, \\ 2\left(\frac{240 - t_1}{40}\right)^2 & \text{if } 220 < t_1 \le 240, \\ 0 & \text{if } t_1 > 240, \end{cases}$$

the fuzzy set $\tilde{B}$ of people with acceptable blood pressure

$$\mu_B(t_2) = \begin{cases} 1 & \text{if } t_2 \leq 130, \\ 1 - 2\left(\frac{t_2-130}{40}\right)^2 & \text{if } 130 < t_2 \leq 150, \\ 2\left(\frac{170-t_2}{40}\right)^2 & \text{if } 150 < t_2 \leq 170, \\ 0 & \text{if } t_2 > 170, \end{cases}$$

and the fuzzy set $\tilde{C}$ of people with adequate weight

$$\mu_C(t_3) = \begin{cases} 0 & \text{if } t_3 \leq 60, \\ 2\left(\frac{t_3-60}{25}\right)^2 & \text{if } 60 < t_3 \leq 72.5, \\ 1 - 2\left(\frac{85-t_3}{25}\right)^2 & \text{if } 72.5 < t_3 \leq 85, \\ 1 & \text{if } 85 < t_3 \leq 110, \\ 1 - 2\left(\frac{t_3-110}{20}\right)^2 & \text{if } 110 < t_3 \leq 120, \\ 2\left(\frac{130-t_3}{20}\right)^2 & \text{if } 120 < t_3 \leq 130, \\ 0 & \text{if } t_3 > 130. \end{cases}$$

The set D of nonsmokers is crisp and

$$\mu_D(t_4) = \begin{cases} 1 & \text{if } t_4 = 0, \\ 0 & \text{otherwise.} \end{cases}$$

The fuzzy set $\tilde{P}$ of preferred risks is then defined as

$$\tilde{P} = \tilde{A} \cap \tilde{B} \cap \tilde{C} \cap D;$$

i.e., for $\mathbf{x} = (t_1, t_2, t_3, t_4)$

$$\mu_P(\mathbf{x}) = \min\left(\mu_A(t_1), \mu_B(t_2), \mu_C(t_3), \mu_D(t_4)\right).$$

A possibility of using other operators defining the fuzzy intersection is then discussed. Finally, it is suggested that in the real life application, an appropriate α-cut of $\tilde{P}$ be chosen as the crisp set of preferred risks.

The derivation of the concept of a preferred risk by Lemaire (1990) presented above is a very simple, direct application of fuzzy set-theoretic concepts. We would like to propose a slightly more involved alternative to it. Of course one should always remember that although more complicated methods may be more powerful, simplicity is a value, especially in applications.

Recall the example of a shopper's approximate reasoning presented before. As we said, fuzzy sets based expert systems model this style of reasoning. Underwriting decisions, especially for medical coverage, are not unlike the decision of the shopper. The main feature of it is that both the inputs and the outputs of such expert systems are fuzzy. Just as in the Lemaire's derivation of the concept of preferred risk, the final step of the algorithm is usually a "defuzzifier"; i.e., a specification of the process in which the fuzzy output is turned into a non-fuzzy (crisp) real-life decision. For Lemaire (1990), as stated above, it was the choice of the appropriate α-cut.

Suppose now that we allow the inputs to be of the form: "applicant's level of cholesterol in the blood is almost high, approximately 210 mg/dl," or "applicant exercises more or less regularly, at least two times a week." This will, of course, correspond more precisely to many situations encountered in real applications for insurance. In such a situation we often need to reason in the manner similar to the "shopper's thinking", or resembling the medical statement (8).

Fuzzy expert systems, based on *fuzzy controllers* provide tools which allow mathematical models for approximate reasoning. As this is precisely the most successful application area for fuzzy sets, there is an enormous body of literature on the subject. Fuzzy logic used in controllers originates in the works of Zadeh (1968, 1973, 1975, 1975, 1975). The first practical fuzzy controller was introduced by Mamdami (1974). Other works which may be referred to include Baldwin (1979), Baldwin and Guild (1980), Baldwin and Pilsworth (1980), Bandler and Kohout (1980), Blishun (1987), Cao, Kandel and Li (1989a, 1989b), Gaines (1976), Gainer and Shaw (1986), Giles (1979, 1982), Gupta, Kandel, Bandler and Kiszka (1985), Gupta and Sanchez (1983), Gupta, Saridis and Gaines (1977), Gupta and Yamakawa (1988), Kacprzyk and Yager (1985), Kickert (1979), Mizumoto and Zimmerman (1982), Nowakowska (1979), Ohand and Bandler (1987), Sanchez and Zadeh (1987), Schmucker (1984), Sugeno (1985), Sugeno and Nishida (1985), Zimmerman, Zadeh and Gaines (1984).

We have given the most general description of fuzzy inference rules, based on the use of T-norms and T-conorms, in Chapter 1. We will now discuss them in a simpler setting, and provide some intuitive justification for their construction.

The purpose of controllers is to compute values of action variables from observation of state variables under control. The relation between state variables and action variables is viewed as a set of logical rules. When this relation is known only qualitatively, fuzzy inference rules may be stated to implement an approximate reasoning strategy. An example of such a rule is the medical statement (8).

Consider a rule of the form:

$$\text{If } X \text{ is } A_i,$$

$$\text{then if } Y \text{ is } B_j, \tag{9}$$

$$\text{then } Z \text{ is } C_k.$$

Here X, Y, Z are assumed to be *linguistic variables*; i.e., variables whose values are statements in the natural, or artificial, language. We assume that A_i, $i = 1, 2, \ldots, n_1$, are possible values of X, B_j, $j = 1, 2, \ldots, n_2$, are possible values of Y, and C_k, $k = 1, 2, \ldots, n_3$, are possible values of Z. Because of the imprecise structure of natural languages, one can model the truth-value of the statement "X is A_i" as a fuzzy subset of $[0, 1]$, similarly for "Y is B_j", and given those truth values, if a logical rule is constructed, that rule will allow us to compute the truth-value of "Z is C_k" (this being done for fixed parameters i, j, k).

Alternatively, one can also model each statement A_i as a fuzzy subset of a certain underlying universe of discourse, similarly for each B_j, and then construct a rule which would derive a membership function for a statement defined on the same universe of discourse as all C_k's. For such a controller, once it is decided that X is A_i (i.e., "applicant exercises somewhat regularly, at least twice a week"), and Y is B_j (i.e., "applicant has a level of cholesterol of approximately 205"), a membership function would be derived for the statement of the C-type, which could then be compared to the membership functions of C_1, C_2, ..., C_{n_3} in order to reach a conclusion about "Z is C_k."

Dubois and Prade (1980, p. 301, also 1991) and Dubois, Lang, and Prade (1991) discuss the variety of specifications of logical rules used in controllers. Generally speaking, fuzzy controllers are meant to be very "user-specific", as the membership functions and the logical rules applied are derived by consulting human experts handling the problem, and by analyzing the data available.

63

Let us illustrate a transformation of a classical "crisp" logical implication into a fuzzy logic implication. It is fairly common to define the crisp implication $p \Rightarrow q$ by the table

$p\backslash q$	1	0
1	1	0
0	1	1

where 1 denotes truth and 0 denotes falsehood. Alternatively, if we write T for the truth-value of a true statement, and F for the truth-value of a false statement, the table becomes

$p\backslash q$	T	F
T	T	F
F	T	T

$$(10)$$

Allow the set $\{T, F\}$ to be the universe of discourse. If p is true, and we write x for its truth value, then $x = T$. This way, a true statement p has its truth-value identified with the subset P of $\{T, F\}$ consisting of T only; i.e.,

$$\mu_P(x) = \begin{cases} 1 & \text{if } x = T, \\ 0 & \text{if } x = F. \end{cases}$$

Similar set Q can be introduced for q

$$\mu_Q(y) = \begin{cases} 1 & \text{if } y = T, \\ 0 & \text{if } y = F. \end{cases}$$

The table (10) of truth-values of $p \Rightarrow q$ can be viewed as a relation R in the set $\{T, F\}$ (i.e., a subset of $\{T, F\}^2$). The membership function of that (crisp) relation is:

$$\mu_R(x, y) = \begin{cases} 1 & \text{if } x = F, \\ 1 & \text{if } x = T, y = T, \\ 0 & \text{if } x = T, y = F. \end{cases}$$

A logical rule can be defined which would exhibit a subset of $\{T, F\}$ corresponding to the truth-value of q, given the truth-values of p and $p \Rightarrow q$. This corresponds to the classical *modus ponens*:

$$p \Rightarrow q,$$

$$\frac{p}{q.}$$

In fact, if we set

$$\mu_Q(y) = \max_x \min \left(\mu_P(x), \mu_R(x, y) \right),$$

then for a true p,

$$\mu_P(x) = \begin{cases} 1 & \text{if } x = T, \\ 0 & \text{if } x = F, \end{cases}$$

we have

$$\mu_Q(y) = \left\{ \begin{array}{l} \max(1,0) \text{ if } y = T \\ \max(0,0) \text{ if } y = F \end{array} \right\} = \begin{cases} 1 & \text{if } y = T, \\ 0 & \text{if } y = F, \end{cases}$$

i.e., q is true, as in the classical *modus ponens*. On the other hand, if p is false,

$$\mu_P(x) = \begin{cases} 0 & \text{if } x = T, \\ 1 & \text{if } x = F, \end{cases}$$

then

$$\mu_Q(y) = \left\{ \begin{array}{l} \max(0,1) \text{ if } y = T \\ \max(0,1) \text{ if } y = F \end{array} \right\} = \begin{cases} 1 & \text{if } y = T, \\ 1 & \text{if } y = F, \end{cases}$$

so that the truth-value of q is undefined. That result, maybe somewhat strange, is exactly what we want – given the truth of implication $p \Rightarrow q$ and falsehood of p, we can make no statement of q.

The above illustration gives an insight into the idea underlying the *compositional rule of inference* of Zadeh (1975). Given a rule of the form

$$\text{If } X_1 \text{ is } A_{i_1},$$

$$\text{and } X_2 \text{ is } A_{i_2},$$

$$\cdots$$

$$\text{and } X_n \text{ is } A_{i_n},$$

$$\text{then } Y \text{ is } B,$$

usually originating from a human expert experience, with each statement of the form "X_k is A_{i_k}" representing a linguistic variable (e.g., X = "blood pressure") being restricted to its value (e.g., A_{i_k} = "low"), with appropriateness of the restriction being described by a membership function $\mu_i : [0,1] \to [0,1]$, we proceed to write the rule as a fuzzy relation; i.e., a fuzzy subset R of $[0,1]^{n+1}$. For example, we can take the following interpretation of implication (Dubois and Prade, 1980, p. 303):

"If each of the statements

$$X_k \text{ is } A_{i_k}$$

is true, then Y is B, otherwise Y is unrestricted."

resulting in

$$\mu_R(x_1, x_2, \ldots, x_n, y) =$$

$$\max\left(\min\left(\mu_1(x_1), \ldots, \mu_n(x_n), \mu_B(y)\right), \min\left(1 - \mu_1(x_1), \ldots, 1 - \mu_n(x_n), 1\right)\right).$$

If now the truth-value of each statement "X_k is A_{i_k}" is given in a form of a fuzzy subset of $[0, 1]$, we use μ_R to arrive at the truth value of "Y is B" as a fuzzy subset of $[0, 1]$

$$\mu_B(y) = \max_{x_1, x_2, \ldots, x_n} \min\left(\mu_1(x_1), \ldots, \mu_n(x_n), \mu_R(x_1, x_2, \ldots, x_n, y)\right).$$

The above rule is referred to as the *Zadeh's Maximin Principle*. Although it is the most studied and the best known rule of inference for fuzzy approximate reasoning, it has been criticized by Mizumoto, Fukami and Tanaka (1979), Tsukamoto (1979), and Mamdami (1977), all of whom proposed other possible definitions of fuzzy inference. We would like to stress again that in applications, fuzzy controllers tend to be "user-specific", and if actuarial applications materialize, it is not unlikely that a different rule may be used to arrive at a decision concerning preferred risk in life insurance than in automobile insurance. Medical underwriting is the area where fuzzy controllers may be applied sooner than anywhere else, given the current rules used in underwriting. One can also envision different expert systems used by different companies to solve exactly the same classification problem – due to differing experiences of the companies, and different business on their books.

In the final paragraph of this chapter we would like to mention two more possible applications of fuzzy sets in classification. One is a direct utilization of the definition of measure of fuzziness. If we classify risks, we generally do know in advance what an "ideal risk" is like. In relation to that "ideal risk", any real risk proposed to be insured, is not perfectly identical to it; i.e., it is a fuzzy "ideal risk". One can, therefore, measure its fitness to be considered a low risk by measuring its fuzziness as an "ideal risk". Empirical studies would, of course, be needed to determine what an "ideal risk" represents, and what measure of fuzziness is most appropriate for this purpose.

The other idea refers to fuzzy measures, and to their more specific forms, the belief measures and plausibility measures. Recall from Chapter 1, that belief and plausibility measures, and other generalized fuzzy measures are used to describe the degree of evidence supporting the claim that a specific element of U belongs to the set A, but not to any special subset of A, or the degree to which we believe that such a claim is warranted. Clearly, belief and plausibility measures defined on the base of our concept of an "ideal risk" can be beneficial in classifying risks.

Chapter 7: ASSUMPTIONS, CONSERVATISM, AND ADJUSTMENT

As Trowbridge (1989) excellently points out:

"In certain situations, it is appropriate that actuaries will tend to be conservative. (...) The reasons are (1) the actuary sees the public's interest as being better served by a conservative approach, and (2) the actuary sees the consequences of error on the conservative side as directly preferable to error in the opposite direction."

What we would like to point out here, however, is that different sets of assumptions could be augmented with their possibility ratings, and as a result of this, an actuary could present a decision maker with more than one set of assumptions (naturally, if one set is presented, it is the conservative one that is chosen), but with a variety of scenarios, each with its own possibility rating. In other words, a fuzzy (multiple-valued) assumption could be a viable alternative to the conservative one, as long as the economic decision maker understands its meaning fully.

Lemaire (1990) gives another possible application of fuzzy sets methodology in that area, a reinsurance problem characterized by its stop-loss deductible solved by applying decision-making techniques with fuzzy goals and constraints.

If X is a set of alternatives, and $\tilde{G}$ is a goal, which is a fuzzy subset of X, and $\tilde{C}$ is a constraint, again a fuzzy subset of X, a decision can be defined as

$$\tilde{D} = \tilde{G} \cap \tilde{C}.$$

Other operators, instead of fuzzy intersection, could also be considered. In the case of multiple goals and constraints we have

$$\tilde{D} = \tilde{G}_1 \cap \ldots \tilde{G}_p \cap \tilde{C}_1 \cap \ldots \cap \tilde{C}_q.$$

The optimizing set K can then be defined as some α-cut of $\tilde{D}$, or the crisp subset of X on which μ_D reaches its maximum value. Lemaire (1990) gives the following example. The reinsurance problem is the one of choosing the program, characterized by its stop-loss deductible, and evaluated by means of two goal variables (probability of ruin, and the coefficient of variation of the retained portfolio) and two constraint variables (the ratio of reinsurance premium to cedent's premium income, and the ratio of deductible to cedent's premium income). He then constructs the membership function for the two goals G_1, G_2, describing their desirability to the cedent, and the two constraints, with similar meaning. The membership function of the decision is simply

$$\mu_D = \min\left(\mu_{G_1}, \mu_{G_2}, \mu_{C_1}, \mu_{C_2}\right).$$

Clearly, an alternative to the above approach would be to create a fuzzy controller using an appropriate rule of inference, as described in Chapter 6. This would, of course, work best if based on the insurer's experience.

One more area where we see a possibly beneficial application of fuzzy approximate reasoning is in analyzing the insurer's risk for which specific statutory contingency reserves may be needed. Recall that a Committee of the Society of Actuaries has identified the following:

C(1) – the risk of asset loss;

C(2) – the risk of pricing insufficiency;

C(3) – the risk of loss due to interest rate swings coupled with asset-liability mismatching.

Not only could each of these risks be best described as a fuzzy concept, but a rule of compositional inference could be used to arrive at an aggregate risk reading, once fuzzy values for C(1), C(2), and C(3) are defined.

Finally, as we have already pointed out in Chapter 5, there is a striking similarity between the reasons why actuaries are conservative and use adjustment instead of direct testing of theory through an experiment and why similar approaches are used in structural engineering and jurisprudence. Smithson (1989) points out how such approaches give rise to possibility of using nonprobabilistic methods of modeling uncertainty.

CLOSING REMARKS

We believe that the methodology developed in the area of fuzzy sets can be successfully applied in several areas of actuarial science. This is still a relatively new methodology, it is constantly changing and improving, but it has proved itself most valuable in creation of expert systems working in situations where information available is imprecise, or vague, and human decision making had been the norm previously. The second valuable application is in situations where the complexity of the problem gets to be excessive, and we learn to appreciate a simple, "rule of thumb" estimate.

The core of actuarial science, based on the classical probabilistic models, will probably not gain much by immediate applications of fuzzy sets in that area. However, there are numerous areas identified in this book, including long-term predictions, classification of risks, underwriting, estimation of risks, where fuzzy sets based controllers not only can be applied, but most likely soon be will be applied. It is important that fuzzy set expert systems are much more "user-specific" than other similar systems. In view of this, we can expect widely differing constructions, even if based on similar rules of compositional inference.

This book is intended as an introduction to the field of fuzzy sets for actuaries, and as a lead into some advanced concepts of fuzzy sets linked to possible actuarial applications. In view of the wide variety of existing specific applications, especially expert system constructions, we give a broad bibliography, hoping that the reader will be able to combine this book's contents with more specific ideas of other works, or the reader's own experience, to develop applications suited for the individual need.

BIBLIOGRAPHY

Adamo, J.M. (1980), Fuzzy decision trees, *Fuzzy Sets and Systems* **4**, pp. 207-219.

Alsina, C., Trillas, E., and Valverde, L. (1983), On some logical connectives for fuzzy set theory, *Journal of Mathematical Analysis and Applications* **93**, pp. 15-26.

Andrews, G.H., and Beekman, J.A. (1987), *Actuarial Projections for the Old-Age, Survivors, and Disability Insurance Program of Social Security in the United States of America*, Actuarial Education and Research Fund, Itasca, Illinois.

Aubin, J.P. (1981), Cooperative fuzzy games, *Mathematics of Operations Research* **6**, pp. 1-13.

Baas, S.M., and Kwakernaak, H. (1977), Rating and ranking of multiple-aspect alternatives using fuzzy sets, *Automatica* **13**, pp. 47-58.

Baldwin, J.F. (1979), New approach to approximate reasoning using a fuzzy logic, *Fuzzy Sets and Systems* **2**, pp. 309-325.

Baldwin, J.F., and Guild, N.C.F. (1980), Feasible algorithms for approximate reasoning using fuzzy logic, *Fuzzy Sets and Systems* **3**. pp. 225-251.

Baldwin, J.F., and Pilsworth, B.W. (1980), Axiomatic approach to implication for approximate reasoning with fuzzy logic, *Fuzzy Sets and Systems* **3**, pp. 193-219.

Bandler, W., and Kohout, L. (1980), Fuzzy power sets and fuzzy implication operators, *Fuzzy Sets and Systems* **4**, pp. 13-30.

Bellman, R., and Zadeh, L.A. (1970), Decision-making in a fuzzy environment, *Management Science* **17**, pp. 141-164.

Bezdek, J.C. (1981), *Pattern Recognition with Fuzzy Objective Function Algorithms*, New York, Plenum Press.

Black, M. (1937), Vagueness: An exercise in logical analysis, *Philosophy of Science* **4**, pp. 427-455.

Blishun, A.F. (1987), Fuzzy learning models in expert systems, *Fuzzy Sets and Systems* **22**, pp. 57-70.

Bock, H.H. (1979), Clusteranalyse mit unscharfen Partitionen, pp. 138-139 in: *Klassifikation und Erkenntnis III*, edited by Bock, H.H., Gesellschaft für Klassifikation, Frankfurt.

Borisov, A., and Krumberg, O. (1983), A theory of possibility for decision making, *Fuzzy Sets and Systems* **9**, pp. 13-24.

Boyle, P.P. (1976), Rates of return as random variables, *Journal of Risk and Insurance* **43**, pp. 693-713.

Bowers, N.L., Gerber, H.U., Hickman, J.C., Jones, D.C., and Nesbitt, C.J. (1986), *Actuarial Mathematics*, Society of Actuaries, Itasca, Illinois.

Buckley, J.J. (1984), The multiple judge, multiple criteria ranking problem: A fuzzy set approach, *Fuzzy Sets and Systems* **13**, pp. 25-37.

Buckley, J.J. (1985), Fuzzy decision making with data: Applications to statistics, *Fuzzy Sets and Systems* **16**, pp. 139-147.

Buckley, J.J. (1985), Fuzzy hierarchical analysis, *Fuzzy Sets and Systems* **17**, pp. 233-247.

Buckley, J.J. (1985), Ranking alternatives using fuzzy numbers, *Fuzzy Sets and Systems* **15**, pp. 21-31.

Buckley, J.J. (1987), Portfolio analysis using possibility distributions, pp. 69-76 in: *Approximate Reasoning in Intelligent System Decision and Control: Proceedings of the International Conference, January 8-10, 1986*, edited by Sanchez, E., and Zadeh, L.A., Pergamon Press, Elmsford, New York.

Buckley, J.J. (1987), The fuzzy mathematics of finance, *Fuzzy Sets and Systems* **21**, pp. 257-273.

Buckley, J.J. (1988), Possibilistic linear programming with triangular fuzzy numbers, *Fuzzy Sets and Systems* **26**, pp. 135-138.

Buckley, J.J. (1989), Fuzzy input-output analysis, *European Journal of Operations Research* **39**, pp. 56-60.

Buckley, J.J. (1989), Solving possibilistic linear programming problems, *Fuzzy Sets and Systems* **31**, pp. 329-341.

Buckley, J.J. (1989), Fuzzy PERT, pp. 103-114 in: *Applications of Fuzzy Set Methodologies in Industrial Engineering*, edited by Evans, G., Karwowski, W., and Wilhelm, M.R., Elsevier, Amsterdam.

Buckley, J.J. (1990), Fuzzy eigenvalues and input-output analysis, *Fuzzy Sets and Systems* **34**, pp. 187-195.

Buckley, J.J. (1991), Solving fuzzy equations in economics and finance, (unpublished).

Butnariu, D. (1978), Fuzzy games: A description of the concept, *Fuzzy Sets and Systems* **1**, pp. 181-192.

Butnariu, D. (1980), Stability and Shapley value for an n-person fuzzy game, *Fuzzy Sets and Systems* **4**, pp. 63-72.

Calzi, M.L. (1990), Towards a general setting for the fuzzy mathematics of finance, *Fuzzy Sets and Systems* **35**, pp. 265-280.

Cao, Z., Kandel, A., and Li, L. (1990), A new model of fuzzy reasoning, *Fuzzy Sets and Systems* **36**, pp. 311-325.

Cao, Z., Kandel, A., and Li, L. (1989), Applicability of some fuzzy implication operators, *Fuzzy Sets and Systems* **31**, pp. 151-186.

Capocelli, R.M., and de Luca, A. (1973), Fuzzy sets and decision theory, *Information and Control* **23**, pp. 446-473.

Chanas, S., and Kamburowski, J. (1981), The use of fuzzy variables in PERT, *Fuzzy Sets and Systems* **5**, pp. 11-20.

Chang, S.S.L. (1977), Application of fuzzy set theory to economics, *Kybernetes: International Journal of Cybernetics and General Systems* **6**, pp. 203-207.

Chen, G., Lee, S., and Yu, E. (1983), Application of fuzzy set theory to economics, pp. 227-305 in: *Advances in Fuzzy Sets, Possibility Theory, and Applications*, edited by Wang, P., Plenum Press, New York.

Civanlar, M.R., and Trunsell, H.J. (1986), Constructing membership functions using statistical data, *Fuzzy Sets and Systems* **18**, pp. 1-13.

Dhaene, J. (1989), Stochastic interest rates and autoregressive integrated moving average processes, *Astin Bulletin* **19**, pp. 131-138.

Dicke, A.A., Bergquist, W., Clancy, R.P., Miller, R.A. III, Panjer, H.H., Peterson, D.M., Watson, C.B.H., and Luckner, W. (1991), *Principles of Actuarial Science*, by the Society of Actuaries Committee of Actuarial Principles, accepted by the Board of Governors in October 1991.

Driankov, D. (1987), An outline of a fuzzy sets approach to decision making with interdependent goals, *Fuzzy Sets and Systems* **21**, pp. 275-288.

Dubois, D., and Prade, H. (1978), Operations on fuzzy numbers, *International Journal of Systems Science* **9**(6), pp. 613-626.

Dubois, D., and Prade, H. (1979), Fuzzy real algebra: Some results, *Fuzzy Sets and Systems* **2**, pp. 327-348.

Dubois, D., and Prade, H. (1980), *Fuzzy Sets and Systems: Theory and Applications*, Academic Press, San Diego, California.

Dubois, D., and Prade, H. (1991), Fuzzy sets in approximate reasoning, Part 1: Inference with possibility distributions, *Fuzzy Sets and Systems* **40**, pp. 143-202.

Dubois, D., Lang, J., and Prade, H. (1991), Fuzzy sets in approximate reasoning, Part 2: Logical approaches, *Fuzzy Sets and Systems* **40**, pp. 203-244.

Dufresne, D. (1988), Moments of pension contributions and fund levels when rates of return are random, *The Journal of the Institute of Actuaries* **115**, pp. 535-544.

Dufresne, D. (1990), The distribution of perpetuity, with applications to risk theory and pension funding, *Scandinavian Actuarial Journal*, pp. 39-79.

Dufresne, D. (1992), On discounting when rates of return are random, *Proceedings of Twenty Fourth International Congress of Actuaries*: **1**, pp. 27-43.

Ellsberg, D. (1961), Risk, ambiguity, and the Savage axioms, *Quarterly Journal of Economics* **75**, pp. 643-669.

Evans, G.W., Karwowski, W., and Wilhelm, M.R. (editors) (1989), *Applications of Fuzzy Set Methodologies in Industrial Engineering*, Elsevier, Amsterdam.

Frees, E.W. (1990), Stochastic life contingencies with solvency considerations, *Transactions of the Society of Actuaries* **42**, pp. 91-129.

Gaines, B.R. (1976), Foundations of fuzzy reasoning, *International Journal of Man-Machine Studies* **8**, pp. 623-688.

Gaines, B.R., and Shaw, M.L.G. (1986), Induction of inference rules for expert systems, *Fuzzy Sets and Systems* **18**, pp. 315-328.

Giles, R. (1976), Lukasiewicz logic and fuzzy set theory, *International Journal of Man-Machine Studies* **6**, pp. 313-327.

Giles, R. (1979), A formal system for fuzzy reasoning, *Fuzzy Sets and Systems* **2**, pp. 233-257.

Giles, R. (1982), Semantics for fuzzy reasoning, *International Journal of Man-Machine Studies* **17**, pp. 401-415.

Goguen, J.A. (1967), L-fuzzy sets, *Journal of Mathematical Analysis and Applications* **18**, pp. 145-174.

Goguen, J.A. (1969), The logic of inexact concepts, *Synthese* **19**, pp. 325-373.

Graham, I. (1991), Fuzzy logic in commercial expert systems – Results and prospects, *Fuzzy Sets and Systems* **40**, pp. 451-472.

Gupta, M.M., Kandel, A., Bandler, W., and Kiszka, J.B. (editors) (1985), *Approximate Reasoning in Expert Systems*, North-Holland Elsevier, Amsterdam.

Gupta, M.M., Ragade, R.K., and Yager, R.R. (editors) (1979), *Advances in Fuzzy Set Theory and Applications*, North-Holland Elsevier, Amsterdam.

Gupta, M.M., and Sanchez, E. (editors) (1983), *Approximate Reasoning in Decision Analysis*, North-Holland Elsevier, Amsterdam.

Gupta, M.M., Saridis, G.N., and Gaines, B.R. (editors) (1977), *Fuzzy Automata and Decision Processes*, North-Holland Elsevier, Amsterdam.

Gupta, M.M., and Qi, J. (1991), Theory of T-norms and fuzzy inference methods, *Fuzzy Sets and Systems* **40**, pp. 431-450.

Gupta, M.M., and Yamakawa, T. (editors) (1988), *Fuzzy Logic in Knowledge-Based Systems*, North-Holland Elsevier, Amsterdam.

Hallin, M. (1977), Etude statistique des facteurs influencant un risque, *Bulletin Association Royale des Actuaires Belges* **72**, pp. 76-92.

Hallin, M., and Ingenbleek, J.F. (1981), Etude statistique de la probabilite de sinistre en assurance automobile, *Astin Bulletin* **12**, pp. 40-56.

Heshmaty, B., and Kandel, A. (1985), Fuzzy linear regression and its applications to forecasting in uncertain environment, *Fuzzy Sets and Systems* **15**, pp. 159-191.

Höhle, U. (1978), Probabilistic uniformization of fuzzy topologies, *Fuzzy Sets and Systems* **1**, pp. 311-332.

Holmblad, L.P., and Ostergaard, J.J. (1983), Control of cement kiln by fuzzy logic, pp. 389-400 in: *Approximate Reasoning in Decision Analysis*, edited by Gupta, M.M., and Sanchez, E., North-Holland Elsevier, Amsterdam.

Jain, R. (1976), Decision-making in the presence of fuzzy variables, *I.E.E.E. Transactions on Systems, Man and Cybernetics* **6**(10), pp. 698-703.

Jain, R. (1977), A procedure for multiple aspect decision-making, *International Journal of Systems Science* **8**(1), pp. 1-7.

Jain, R. (1978), Decision-making in the presence of fuzziness and uncertainty, *Proceedings of the I.E.E.E. Conference on Decision Control, New Orleans*, pp. 1318-1323.

Jajuga, K. (1986), Linear fuzzy regression, *Fuzzy Sets and Systems* **20**, pp. 343-353.

Jones, P.L.K. (1983), *REVEAL's User Manual*, Tymshare Inc.

Kacprzyk, J., and Yager, R.R. (editors) (1985), *Management Decision Support Systems Using Fuzzy Sets and Possibility Theory*, Verlag TUV Rheinland, Cologne.

Kandel, A. (1986), *Fuzzy Mathematical Techniques with Applications*, Addison-Wesley, Reading, Massachussetts.

Kaufmann, A. (1975), *Introduction to the Theory of Fuzzy Subsets, vol. I: Fundamental Theoretical Elements*, Academic Press, New York.

Kellison, S. (1991), *Theory of Interest*, Second Edition, Richard D. Irwin, Boston.

Kickert, W.J. (editor) (1979), *Fuzzy Theories in Decision Making*, Frontiers in Systems Research Series, vol. 3, Martinus Nijhoff, Leiden, The Netherlands.

Klir, G.J., and Folger, T.A. (1988), *Fuzzy Sets, Uncertainty, and Information*, Prentice Hall, Englewood Cliffs, New Jersey.

Kosko, B. (1990), Fuzziness vs. probability, *International Journal of General Systems* **17**, pp. 211-240.

Kosko, B. (1991), *Neural Networks and Fuzzy Systems: A Dynamical Systems Approach to Machine Intelligence*, Prentice Hall, Englewood Cliffs, New Jersey.

Kwakernaak, H. (1978), Fuzzy random variables I: Definitions and terms, *Information Science* **15**, pp. 1-29.

Kwakernaak, H. (1979), Fuzzy random variables II: Algorithms and examples for the discrete case, *Information Science* **17**, pp. 253-278.

Lazarescu, A. E., and Philips, C.H. (1992), The Society of Actuaries and antitrust compliance, Supplement to *The Actuary*, January 1992.

Lebesgue, H. (1902), Intégrale, longeur, aire, *Annali di Matematica Pura et Applicada* (3)**7**, pp. 231-359.

Lemaire, J. (1990), Fuzzy insurance, *Astin Bulletin* **20**(1), pp. 33-55.

de Luca, A., and Termini, S. (1972), A definition of nonprobabilistic entropy in the setting of fuzzy sets theory, *Information and Control* **20**, pp. 301-312.

Łukasiewicz, J. (1920), O logice trójwartościowej (On three-valued logic) (in Polish), *Ruch Filozoficzny* **5**, pp. 169-171.

Łukasiewicz, J. (1930), Philosophische Bemerkungen zu mehrwertigen Systemen des Aussagenkalküls, *Comptes Rendus des Séances de la Societe des Sciences et des Lettres de Varsovie* Cl. iii, **23**, pp. 51-72.

Łukasiewicz, J. (1953), A system of modal logic, *The Journal of Computing Systems* **1**, pp. 111-149.

Łukasiewicz, J. (1954), Arithmetic and modal logic, *The Journal of Computing Systems* **1**, pp. 213-219.

Mamdami, E.H. (1974), Application of fuzzy algorithms for control of simple dynamic plant, *Proceedings of the Institute of Electrical Engineers* **121**, pp. 1585-1588.

Mamdani, E.H. (1977), Application of fuzzy logic to approximate reasoning using linguistic system, *I.E.E.E. Transactions on Computing* C-**26**, pp.1182-1191.

Mathieu-Nicot, B. (1986), Fuzzy expected utility, *Fuzzy Sets and Systems* **20**, pp. 163-173.

Mathieu-Nicot, B. (1990), Determination and interpretation of the fuzzy utility of an act in an uncertain environment, pp. 90-97 in: *Multiperson Decision Making Using Fuzzy Sets and Possibility Theory*, edited by Kacprzyk, J., and Fedrizzi, M., Kluwer Academic Publishers, Dordrecht, The Netherlands.

Menger, K. (1949), Statistical metrics, *Proceedings of the National Academy of Sciences of the United States of America* **28**, pp. 535-537.

McCall, S. (editor) (1967), *Polish Logic 1920-1939*, Clarendon Press, Oxford.

Mizumoto, M., Fukami, S., and Tanaka, K. (1979), Some methods of fuzzy reasoning, pp. 117-136 in: *Advances in Fuzzy Set Theory and Applications*, edited by Gupta, M.M., Ragade, R.K., and Yager, R.R., North-Holland Elsevier, Amsterdam.

Mizumoto, M., and Zimmerman, H.J. (1982), Comparison of fuzzy reasoning methods, *Fuzzy Sets and Systems* **8**, pp. 253-283.

Nowakowska, M. (1979), New ideas in decision theory, *International Journal of Man-Machine Studies* **11**, pp. 213-234.

Ohand, K.W., and Bandler, W. (1987), Properties of fuzzy implication operators, *International Journal of Approximate Reasoning* **1**, pp. 273-285.

Ostergaard, J.J. (1977), Fuzzy logic control of a heat exchanger system, in: *Fuzzy Automata and Decision Processes*, edited by Gupta, M.M., Saridis, G.N., and Gaines, B.R., North-Holland Elsevier, Amsterdam.

Panjer, H.H., and Bellhouse, D.R. (1980), Stochastic modelling of interest rates with applications to life contingencies, *Journal of Risk and Insurance* **47**, pp. 91-110.

Panjer, H.H., and Bellhouse, D.R. (1981), Stochastic modelling of interest rates with applications to life contingencies, Part II, *Journal of Risk and Insurance* **48**, pp. 628-637.

Phlips, L. (1983), *The Economics of Price Discrimination*, Cambridge University Press, Cambridge.

Pigou, A.C. (1920), *The Economics of Welfare*, Macmillan and Company, Ltd., London.

Pollard, J.H. (1971), On fluctuating interest rates, *Bulletin de l'Association Royale des Actuaires Belges* **66**, pp. 68-94.

Ponsard, C. (1979), On the imprecision of consumer's spatial preferences, *R.S.A. Papers* **42**, pp. 59-71.

Ponsard, C.(1981), An application of fuzzy subsets theory to the analysis of the consumer's spatial preferences, *Fuzzy Sets and Systems* **5**, pp. 235-244.

Ponsard, C. (1982), Producer's spatial equilibrium with a fuzzy constraint, *European Journal of Operations Research* **10**, pp. 302-313.

Ponsard, C. (1985), Fuzzy sets in economics: Foundations of soft decision theory, in: *Management Decision Support Systems Using Fuzzy Sets and Possibility Theory*, edited by Kacprzyk, J., and Yager, R.R., Verlag TUV Rheinland, Cologne.

Ponsard, C. (1988), Fuzzy mathematical models in economics, *Fuzzy Sets and Systems* **28**, pp. 273-283.

Post, E.L. (1921), A general theory of elementary propositions, *The American Journal of Mathematics* **43**, pp. 163-185.

Prior, A.N. (1953), On propositions neither necessary nor impossible, *The Journal of Symbolic Logic* **18**.

Puri, M., and Ralescu, D. (1982), A possibility measure is not a fuzzy measure, *Fuzzy Sets and Systems* **7**, pp. 311-313.

Puri, M., and Ralescu, D. (1986), Fuzzy random variables, *Journal of Mathematical Analysis and Applications* **114**, pp. 409-422.

Sanchez, E., and Zadeh, L.A. (editors) (1987), *Approximate Reasoning in Intelligent Systems*, Pergamon Press, Oxford, England.

Schmucker, K. (1984), *Fuzzy Sets, Natural Language Computations, and Risk Analysis*, Computer Science Press, New York.

Schwartz, T.J. (1990), Fuzzy systems in the real world, *AI Expert*, August 1990, pp. 29-35.

Schweizer, B., and Sklar, A. (1982), *Probabilistic Metric Spaces*, North-Holland Elsevier, Amsterdam.

Smithson, M. (1989), *Ignorance and Uncertainty: Emerging Paradigms*, Springer-Verlag, New York.

Stigler, G. (1987), *Theory of Price*, 4th Edition, Macmillan, New York.

Stiglitz, J. (1977), Monopoly, non-linear pricing, and imperfect information: The insurance market, *Review of Economic Studies* **44**, pp. 407-430.

Sugeno, M. (1985), An introductory survey of fuzzy control, *Information Sciences* **36**, pp. 59-83.

Sugeno, M., and Nishida, M., Fuzzy control of model car, *Fuzzy Sets and Systems* **16**, pp. 103-113.

Trowbridge, C.L. (1989), *Fundamental Concepts of Actuarial Science*, Actuarial Education and Research Fund, Schaumburg, Illinois.

Tsukamoto, Y. (1979), An approach to fuzzy reasoning method, pp. 137-149 in: *Advances in Fuzzy Set Theory and Applications*, edited by Gupta, M.M. Ragade, R.K., and Yager, R.R., North-Holland Elsevier, Amsterdam.

Wang, J.H., Littschwager, J.M., and Raz, T. (1989), Equipment life estimation using fuzzy set theory, pp. 197-211 in: *Applications of Fuzzy Set Methodologies in Industrial Engineering*, edited by Evans, G., Karwowski, W., and Wilhelm, M.R., Elsevier, Amsterdam.

Wang, P. (editor) (1983), *Advances in Fuzzy Sets, Possibility Theory, and Applications*, Plenum Press, New York.

Ward, T.L., Fuzzy discounted cash flow analysis, pp. 213-221 in: *Applications of Fuzzy Set Methodologies in Industrial Engineering*, edited by Evans, G., Karwowski, W., and Wilhelm, M.R., Elsevier, Amsterdam.

Waters, H.R. (1978), The moments and distributions of actuarial functions, *Journal of the Institute of Actuaries* **105**, pp. 61-75.

Watson, S.R., Weiss, J.J., and Donnell, M. (1979), Fuzzy design analysis, *I.E.E.E. Trans. Syst., Man Cybern.* **9**(1), pp. 1-9.

Wilkie, A.D. (1976), The rate of interest as a stochastic process: Theory and applications, *Proceedings of the Twentieth International Congress of Actuaries* **1**, pp. 325-338.

Windham, M.P. (1982), Cluster validity for the fuzzy c-means clustering algorithms, *IEEE Transactions on PA and MI* **4**, pp. 358-359.

Van Eeghen, J., Greup, E.K., and Nijssen, J.A. (1983), *Rate Making*, Surveys of Actuarial Studies, No. 2, Nationale-Nederlanden N.V., Rotterdam.

Varian, H. (1989), Price discrimination, chapter 10 in: *Handbook of Industrial Organization*, vol. I, edited by Schmalensee, R., and Willig, R.D., North-Holland Elsevier, Amsterdam.

Von Wright, G.H. (1967), *Logical Studies* (Second Edition), Routledge and Kegan Paul Ltd., London, England.

Yager, R. (1977), Fuzzy decision making including unequal objectives, *Fuzzy Sets and Systems* **1**, pp. 87-95.

Yager, R. (1979), On the measure of fuzziness and negation, Part I: Membership in the unit interval, *International Journal of General Systems* **5**, pp. 221-229.

Yager, R., and Basson, D. (1975), Decision making with fuzzy sets, *Decision Sciences* **6**, pp. 590-600.

Zadeh, L.A. (1965), Fuzzy sets, *Information and Control* **8**, pp. 338-353.

Zadeh, L.A. (1968), Fuzzy algorithms, *Information and Control* **12**, pp. 94-102.

Zadeh, L.A. (1973), Outline of a new approach to the analysis of complex systems and decision processes, *IEEE Transactions on Systems, Man and Cybernetics* SMC-**3**, pp. 28-44.

Zadeh, L.A. (1975), Calculus of fuzzy restrictions, in: *Fuzzy Sets and Their Applications to Cognitive and Decision Processes*, edited by Zadeh, L.A., Fu, K.S., Tanaka, K., and Shimura, K., Academic Press, New York.

Zadeh, L.A. (1975), Fuzzy logic and approximate reasoning, *Synthese* **30**, 407-428.

Zadeh, L.A. (1975), The concept of linguistic variable and its application to approximate reasoning (Parts 1-3), *Information Sciences* **8**, pp. 199-249, and pp. 301-357, **9**, pp. 43-80.

Zadeh, L.A. (1978), Fuzzy sets as a basis for the theory of possibility, *Fuzzy Sets and Systems* **1**, pp. 3-28.

Zadeh, L.A. (1978), A theory of approximate reasoning, *Machine Intelligence* **19**.

Zadeh, L.A. (1983), A computational approach to fuzzy quantifiers in natural languages, *Computers and Mathematics with Applications* **9**(1), pp. 149-184.

Zadeh, L.A. (1983), The role of fuzzy logic in the management of uncertainty in expert systems, *Fuzzy Sets and Systems* **11**, pp. 199-227.

Zadeh, L.A. (1990), The birth and evolution of fuzzy logic, in: *Proceedings of NAFIPS'90, June 6-8, 1990*, edited by Turksen, I.B., pp. 13-21.

Zadeh, L.A., Fu, K.S., Tanaka, K., and Shimura, K., (editors) (1975), *Fuzzy Sets and Their Applications to Cognitive and Decision Processes*, Academic Press, New York.

Zimmermann, H.J. (1991), *Fuzzy Set Theory and its Applications*, Second Edition, Kluwer Academic Publishers, Boston, Massachusetts.

Zimmerman, H.J. (1987), *Fuzzy Sets, Decision Making and Expert Systems*, Kluwer Academic Publishers, Boston, Massachusetts.

Zimmerman, H.J., Zadeh, L.A., and Gaines, B.R. (editors) (1984), *Fuzzy Sets and Decision Analysis*, TIMS Studies in the Management Sciences, vol. 20, North-Holland Elsevier, Amsterdam.

INDEX

In this index page numbers are given in italics if they represent the definition or the main source of information about the item indexed.

ignorance, 5.

inflation, 6, 28–29.

    risk premium, 32.

interest rate, 30–32, 41–43, 46.

    fuzzy, *30*, 32, 41, 46.

Kolmogorov's axiomatic approach to probability, 6.

L–R-type fuzzy number, *40*, 42.

    addition of, *41*.

    mean value of, *40*.

    multiplication of, *42*.

    spread of, *40*.

languages, 7.

    natural, 7.

    programming, 8.

leveraged buyout, 46.

life contingencies, 28.

life expectancy, 49, 60.

linear programming, 27.

linguistic variable, *20*, 64.

logic,

    Aristotelian, 9, 60.

    Boolean, 9, 60.

    modal, 9.

    multivalued, 9.

    three-valued, *9*.

marginal cost, 48.

market power, 48.

maximin principle, 26, *67*.

measure of fuzziness, *23*, 24, 67.

measure of fuzziness (*continued*)

    entropy, *23*.

    Yager's, *24*.

measure theory, 21.

membership function, *12*, 20, 32, 35, 38, 52–54.

modus ponens, *65*, 66.

monopoly, 48, 50.

moving average process, 28.

negation function, *19*.

    strict, *19*.

    involutive, *19*.

net single premium, 30–38.

    fuzzy, *30*, 32.

    for pure endowment, 30.

nonforfeiture benefits, 32.

nonlinear pricing, *48*.

nonspecifity, 6.

normal fuzzy set, *13*.

operations research, 27.

opportunity cost, 48.

pattern recognition, *51*, 59.

    fuzzy, *51*, 59.

pension funding, 28.

perfect competition, 50.

plausibility measure, *22*, 67.

political decision makers, 47.

Popperian scientist, 45.

possibility, 26.

    distribution, 46.